Hamlyn all-colour paperbacks

S. Pe

Se

illustrated by James Nicholls

Hamlyn · London
Sun Books · Melbourne

FOREWORD

Seashells are among the most attractive and durable of all natural objects and are easy to collect and store. Some are almost impossible to obtain and a few are worth a lot of money, but the great majority of them are not difficult to come by. This book gives an idea of the variety and abundance of the different kinds of seashells now existing in the world's seas. It does not concentrate on those which are the especial favourites of established collectors, since that aspect of the subject is well covered by numerous modern handbooks. By spreading the load evenly it has been possible to illustrate and discuss numerous molluscan groups which are ignored by most writers of semi-popular books on shells. Special attention is given to those molluscs which are eaten by humans or whose shells are utilized by them in various ways.

Nearly all the illustrations have been drawn from actual specimens and the stated size of each shell is the largest dimension (including spines) obtainable from the shell depicted. The accompanying locality information gives the known range of the species. Scientific names are given for every species mentioned, and where it exists a popular name is given also. Names of superfamilies (ending in -acea) are added after vernacular group names.

The fine shell collection in the National Museum of Wales has provided most of the illustrative material. The British Museum (Natural History) lent several shells and artifacts, and Mr H. C. Gay lent a shell of *Scalenostoma lamberti*. Without this material help the book could not have come to fruition. I should also like to acknowledge my debt to Mr James Nicholls whose willingness to co-operate with me in every way deserves to be recorded. Of course I hope that those who buy this little book will read it, but Mr Nicholls has given them several hundred reasons for not doing so.

S.P.D.

Published by The Hamlyn Publishing Group Limited
London · New York · Sydney · Toronto
Hamlyn House, Feltham, Middlesex, England
In association with Sun Books Pty. Ltd. Melbourne

Copyright © The Hamlyn Publishing Group Limited 1971

ISBN 0 600 37908 6
Phototypeset by Filmtype Services Limited, Scarborough
Colour separations by Schwitter Limited, Zurich
Printed in Holland by Smeets, Weert

CONTENTS

INTRODUCING SEASHELLS

What are seashells?

It may surprise some persons to learn that seashells are the cast-off coverings of soft-bodied creatures. Surprising because, on the beach, where most of us make our first acquaintance with them, nearly all of those we pick up are quite empty and lifeless. A seashell is to the animal which made it what the external carapace is to the crab and the internal skeleton to the human body. Deprived of its shell the mollusc (for that is the correct name of our soft-bodied creature) would be shapeless, unsupported and unprotected.

Anyone can recognize seashells on sight, but some non-molluscan objects may be mistaken for them. The valves of lamp shells (brachiopods) resemble bivalved seashells, and barnacles may be mistaken for limpets. Both were once thought to be molluscs because of these resemblances. Tubes secreted by annelid worms *(Serpula)* are often seen cemented to other objects – frequently to scallop shells – and these may be mistaken for the tubes of certain tropical molluscs *(Vermetus, Siphonium)*. Beach flotsam contains the dismembered parts of many other sea creatures which may look like seashells. Conversely, some accessory hard parts of molluscs may be passed over as non-molluscan and experts have been fooled by such objects. A competent zoologist once described a fragment of a scorpion shell *(Lambis)* as the fang of an extinct gigantic snake.

Paradoxically many of the most advanced, most successful molluscs are shell-less (anyone who has seen slugs swarming in a garden after rain can hardly doubt this). Some of these 'naked' molluscs, especially those in the sea, are extremely beautiful but their beauty vanishes when they die or even when they are taken out of the water. It is otherwise with seashells in which an infinite variety of shape and colour is expressed in a more durable manner.

1 European Winkle, *Littorina littorea* L. **2** European Cockle, *Cerastoderma edule* L. **3** Brachiopod, *Terebratella sanguinea* Leach. **4** Barnacle, *Balanus variegatus* Darwin. **5** Annelid worm tube, *Serpula*. **6** Sea urchin, *Parechinus angulosus* Leske. All drawn to scale

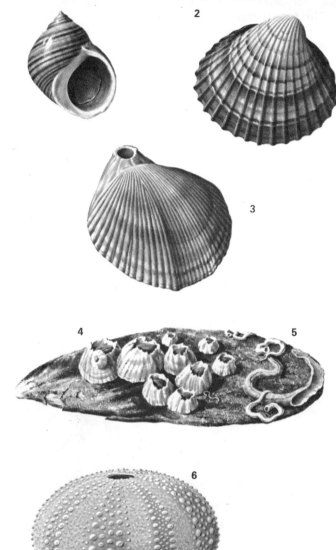

Classes of molluscs

Over 100,000 molluscs are believed to exist today, which makes the Mollusca – the major group, or phylum, to which they belong – the second largest in the animal kingdom (the phylum Arthropoda – insects, spiders, crabs, etc. – is easily the largest). Of these about 50,000 live in the sea including representatives of each of the six sub-groups, or classes, into which the phylum is subdivided. Monoplacophora (gastroverms) – 5 species, all marine. Amphineura (chitons) – about 500 species, all marine. Scaphopoda (tusk shells) – about 300 species, all marine. Cephalopoda (squids, octopuses) – about 400 species, all marine. Bivalvia (bivalves) – about 20,000 species, marine and freshwater. Gastropoda (snails) – about 80,000 species, marine, freshwater and land.

Class Monoplacophora: the most primitive of all living molluscs. Their bodies are segmented and the internal organs and gills are paired. They have no eyes or tentacles, but they do have a row of teeth (the radula). The fragile shell resembles that of the limpet. Unknown to science until the 1950s all the species have been found in very deep water. Their

Neopilina adenensis Tebble; 1·07 cm; Aden, deep water

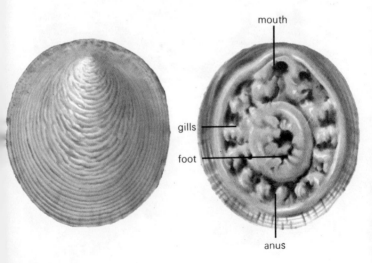

mouth

gills

foot

anus

6

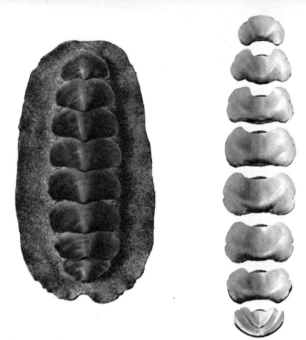

A chiton, *Guildingia obtecta* Pilsbry, in the natural state (6·8 cm) and with the valves separated; N. Zealand

discovery indicates how little we know of life in the abyssal depths of the world's seas.

Class Amphineura: known as chitons or coat-of-mail shells these molluscs are far removed from the popular conception of seashells. They have a series of eight shelly plates arranged serially and held together by a leathery girdle. They lack true eyes and tentacles but light-sensitive organs are present in the integument of the shelly plates. The teeth of the radula are well developed in most species. Sometimes the shelly plates are large and thick, but they may be so reduced in some species as to be almost lost in the animal's skin. The girdle may be ornamented with spines, bristles or knobs. Chitons can curl up like hedgehogs if removed from the rocks on which they are usually found. A few species are recorded from deep water but most are found close to the shore.

1 *Argonauta hians* Lightfoot, showing female in egg case (not a true shell); 8·0 cm (egg case only); Pan-tropical. 2 A deep-sea cephalopod, *Mastigoteuthis flammea* Chun; 8·0 cm. 3 *Antalis entalis* L., showing animal protruding from large end; 3·5 cm (shell only); Boreal-Mediterranean Provs. 4 *Fissidentalium shoplandi* Jousseaume; 7·0 cm; Red Sea. 5 *F. vernedei* Sowerby; 12·2 cm; Japan

Class Scaphopoda: as their popular name – tusk shells – implies these are creatures with shells resembling elephants' tusks. They are headless, eyeless and gill-less, but even these lowly creatures have separate sexes. The shell is hollow from end to end and the narrower end projects obliquely out of the sand into the water. The animal's broad, plug-like foot is protruded from the other end into the sand. A strong radula helps convey the food organisms to the stomach. Some species have been trawled from great depths but most of them are restricted to shallow water.

Class Cephalopoda: includes the largest, most intelligent and most rapacious invertebrates in the world. Nearly all the species are carnivorous and seize their prey with their long, prehensile tentacles and then tear at it with their

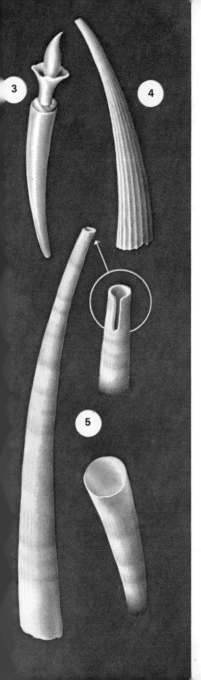

parrot-like beaks. Strong radular teeth complete the work of reducing the prey to a digestible pulp. Cephalopods are strong, alert and fast moving. From a funnel-like process on the underside of their bodies they eject water at high speed and so develop a kind of jet propulsion. Some species also eject clouds of dark fluid when evasive action is necessary and this produces the underwater equivalent of a smoke screen (it can be extracted from the animal and used as a high-quality writing ink too). Many deep-sea forms have evolved light organs, and some surface-dwelling species can change colour to resemble their surroundings. Only the few species of *Nautilus* have external shells, but squids and cuttlefish have internal 'rods' or 'bones' for support. The so-called shell of *Argonauta*, known as the Paper Nautilus, is nothing more than an egg case secreted by the female's two flat 'arms'. The octopus is shell-less. The kraken and other fictional sea monsters may have a real, molluscan foundation. Remains of squids retrieved from whales' stomachs indicate that the sea harbours species more than 18 m long.

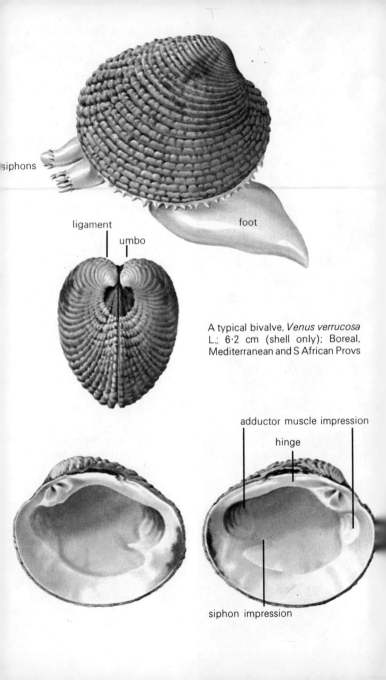

siphons

ligament

umbo

foot

A typical bivalve, *Venus verrucosa*
L.; 6·2 cm (shell only); Boreal,
Mediterranean and S African Provs

adductor muscle impression

hinge

siphon impression

Class Bivalvia (bivalves): known alternatively as Pelecypoda and Lamellibranchia (these names alluding respectively to the hatchet-like foot and plate-like gills characteristic of most bivalves), this class contains cockles, mussels, scallops and many other shells familiar to the beachcomber. Bivalves – meaning two-valved or two-shelled – are headless and lack the radular teeth present in all the other classes. They all have gills which take up a large part of the space inside the valves, for many bivalves feed by filtering food particles from water drawn in over the ciliated gills. The large 'foot' constitutes a large part of the animal and takes on a variety of shapes and functions in the different groups. A large, muscular foot indicates a burrower, and a poorly developed one indicates that its possessor burrows little if at all. Some species are fixed in one place for most of their lives and these have a much-reduced foot. Some species spin a 'byssus', a kind of silken anchor. Some, notably scallops, can flit around in the water like butterflies, and in these the muscles attaching the animal to the shell are well developed and powerful. There are usually two siphons. Through one of them food is taken in and through the other waste products are expelled. Long siphons indicate that the animal leads a burrowing existence, while short ones indicate that it leads a non-burrowing existence.

The shells of many bivalves are thin and fragile but others, such as that of the Giant Clam of the Pacific, are so thick and heavy that they cannot move. Usually there are interlocking 'teeth' on the inside edges of the valves near to the ligament, uniting and strengthening the valves. Impressed on the inside of the valves are the marks made by the animal's muscles and siphons, and these give valuable clues to its way of life and help us to identify it. The foot of the living animal always protrudes anteriorly and the siphons are always directed posteriorly. The two valves are obviously different and can usually be distinguished as right-hand or left-hand valves. In most bivalves the external ligament lies behind the umbones. Hold the valve in the right hand with the umbo uppermost and the outside against your palm: you have a right valve if the external ligament (or the hollow it once filled) is between the umbo and you.

Class Gastropoda (gastropods): easily the largest and most diversified class of molluscs (the name implies that an animal of this class crawls on its stomach). All snail-like and most slug-like creatures are gastropods and they can be found in the deepest oceans, in freshwater lakes and rivers, in forests and deserts, and even on bare mountain tops. Few gastropods stay fixed in one place, and some are surprisingly active and can leap or swim. Such adaptable creatures are certain to assume many different forms, and they exhibit an amazing variety of size, shape and colour. Most have a one-piece (or univalve) shell and this is usually coiled in a right-handed (or dextral) spiral and contains the vital organs. Some are normally coiled in a left-handed (or sinistral) spiral, and a few terrestrial gastropods have shells coiled either way. Sinistral (or dextral) freaks of normally dextral (or sinistral) shells are found occasionally and some are highly prized by collectors. Such monstrosities occur more often in some species than in others. It is not remarkable for a large museum to have a drawer full of sinistral European Whelks *(Buccinum undatum* L.*)*. By contrast, it is doubtful if all the world's museums have more than a dozen sinistral specimens between them of the equally common European Winkle *(Littorina littorea* L.*)*.

On the foot of some species there is a horny or shelly process (the operculum) which acts like a door to plug up the shell's aperture when the animal withdraws into it. Such operculated molluscs (or prosobranchs) have gills and are primarily aquatic, but there are many terrestrial forms as well. Most of those without an operculum are air breathers (or pulmonates), breathing by means of a lung-like organ, and include the highly evolved land snails and land slugs. The radula takes on many different forms in this class and is sometimes used as a basis of classification. Tentacles and eyes are usually present, and some species have a well-developed siphon.

1 A typical gastropod, the European Whelk, *Buccinum undatum* L.; 10·0 cm (shell only); Boreal Prov. **2** Shell with right-handed spiral, aperture on the right. **3** Shell with left-handed spiral, aperture on the left

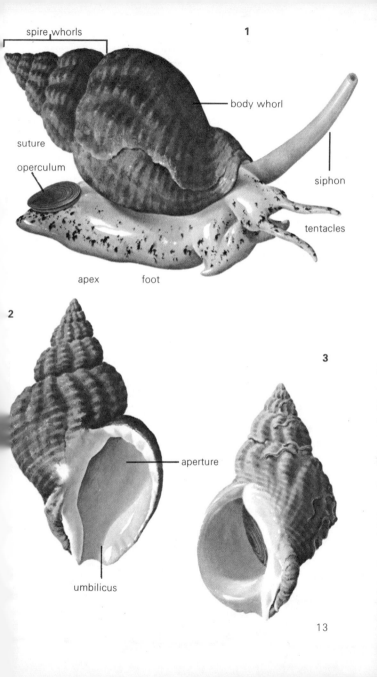

1

spire whorls

body whorl

suture

operculum

siphon

tentacles

apex   foot

2

3

aperture

umbilicus

13

Biology
Reproduction and development

Molluscs have exploited many of the sexual permutations open to animals. Pulmonates and some other gastropods are hermaphrodites, which is to say that each individual has a complete set of male and female reproductive organs, fertilization between them being mutual. A few species are male when young and female when mature. Most of the remaining molluscs have separate sexes and do not change their sexual roles throughout their lives. In many species the shells of females are conspicuously larger than those of the males.

The eggs of most bivalves, chitons and tusk shells are extruded into the water quite unprotected. Some gastropod eggs develop inside the mother, or, as in the cowries, are hatched by being sat on for several days. Other gastropod eggs are protected by burial or by enclosure within gelatinous or

1 Shell of *Lambis lambis* L.; male *(above)* 13·0 cm, female 15·0 cm; Indo-Pacific Prov. **2** Egg capsules on shell of *Cantharus macrospira* Berry; 4·0 cm (shell only); Lower California. **3** Egg capsule *(above)* and veliger larva of the European Winkle, highly magnified

1

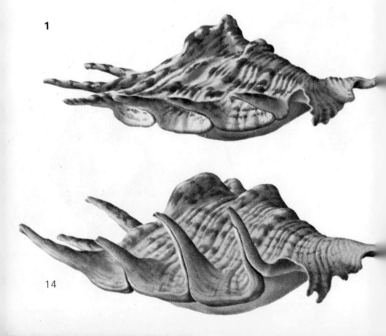

horny capsules. These capsules vary greatly in different families. Some eggs are deposited singly but the majority of marine molluscs deposit many eggs, in clusters or strings, and usually attach them firmly to other objects. Some of those species which do not provide protective coverings for their eggs may each shed millions of them into the water each year. Out of each million only one or two reach maturity.

The fertilized eggs of most marine molluscs change into trochophore larvae, and a few hours later into veliger larvae. It is at the veliger stage that the mollusc is most vulnerable and it is usual for many eggs to be produced to offset the high mortality rate. The veliger's short, free-swimming life explains why far more molluscs are found in shallow coastal seas than on the sea floor beyond the continental shelves of major land masses. The gastropod veliger undergoes torsion, twisting in such a way that the shell and the internal organs are turned 180 degrees while the head and foot remain where they are. This means that the anal and reproductive orifices end up at the front of the mollusc rather than at the rear.

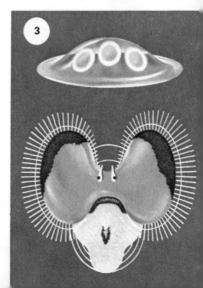

Feeding

Molluscs are herbivorous, carnivorous, or omnivorous. Some, such as the squids, are cannibals, and a few marine snails are parasitic in or on other creatures. Sea water is charged with tiny particles of vegetable or animal food and many marine molluscs are equipped to extract this suspended food (hence they are often called suspension-feeders). The siphons and gills of most bivalves are used to channel the food-laden water or mud to the animals' mouths. Most gastropods obtain their food by scraping plants, or rocks, wood and other

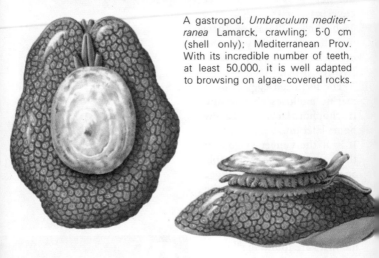

A gastropod, *Umbraculum mediter-ranea* Lamarck, crawling; 5·0 cm (shell only); Mediterranean Prov. With its incredible number of teeth, at least 50,000, it is well adapted to browsing on algae-covered rocks.

objects on which food organisms can be found. Chitons browse on algae-covered rocks, and tusk shells feed on tiny unicellular organisms which they pick up on the sticky ends of filaments (known as captacula). Cephalopods chase their prey, usually fishes, seize it in their tentacles, and bite or tear it to pieces. Those human beings who have survived attacks by squids know only too well that they are also partial to human flesh. Some carnivorous marine snails bore holes in the shells of other molluscs and suck out the succulent soft parts of their victims. A few gastropods can force open the two valves of oysters and other bivalves to make a meal of them, and a tooth-like process on the lip of their own shells helps them gain a purchase.

Movement
Because they have no legs molluscs cannot run or walk. Almost every other kind of animal locomotion is adopted by them: crawling, gliding, burrowing, leaping, swimming. The gastropod foot (which is in no way analogous to the mammalian foot) is most often used for crawling – sliding

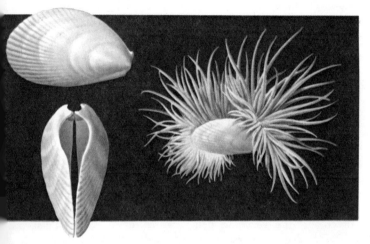

A bivalve, *Lima hians* Gmelin, swimming by means of tentacles; 3·0 cm (shell only); Boreal-Mediterranean Provs

would be a better term – but sometimes it is used for swimming purposes, and some gastropods, particularly those with heavy and spiny shells, leap along by using the muscular foot as a catapult. Most bivalves, many gastropods and most scaphopods burrow downwards or travel horizontally just under the surface of the mud or sand. Some gastropods just allow themselves to drift on the sea surface, and the most abundant molluscs in the world, numerically speaking, are pteropods, insubstantial creatures which flit about aimlessly in the upper levels of the sea.

Composition

Most shells are composed of several differing layers and these layers can be seen easily in fractured shells. The outermost layer, the periostracum, is usually very thin and pigmented. Underneath there are usually three much thicker layers, known respectively as the outer prismatic, the crossed lamellar, and the inner porcellaneous. Almost always the crossed lamellar layer is the thickest of all, and the makers of shell cameos take advantage of this, the background of their cameos being formed nearly always of the inner porcellaneous layer. The periostracum, composed principally of a substance called conchiolin, is relatively soft and pliable (the operculum in many species is also made largely of the same substance). The main ingredient of the other layers is calcium carbonate (a substance vital to molluscs). To strengthen the shell the layers are deposited in such a way that they resemble a block of ply-wood with the crossed lamellar layer the thickest. Usually the mantle, which secretes the shell-building substances, does not extend far beyond the edge of the shell, but some molluscs, notably cowries, extend it right over the shell; this results in a highly polished and smooth surface.

Pigmentation

The molluscan mantle deposits pigment at the same time as it deposits shell matter. Some shells are notoriously variable in colour, the variation being caused by different diets, different degrees of water salinity, and other, more obscure factors. It is necessary to distinguish between these chemical colours and those which are purely physical. Many shells have mother-of-pearl linings which produce beautiful displays of iridescence in certain lights. This is because the light rays are reflected differentially as they pass through the inner porcellaneous layer. Once the pigment has been deposited the animal is powerless to change it, since the shell, together with the incorporated pigment, is virtually dead. Many molluscs develop beautifully patterned shells – only to cover them up with an unsightly and opaque periostracum. Long ago it was thought that beautiful shells are so covered for the sole purpose of giving us the pleasure of discovering the beauties lying underneath!

Cassis madagascariensis Lamarck; 21·0 cm; Caribbean Prov. The cameo-cutter has utilized the layered structure of the shell to good effect.

Growth

The animal continually adds new material to its shell at the mantle edge, the growth rate being determined by several factors, the principal one being temperature. Warm waters favour shell growth and so it is in the tropics that we find the larger shelled molluscs. In gastropods shell growth spirals away from the tiny apex; in bivalves it proceeds away from each umbo simultaneously. Permanent evidence of past growth can be seen on many shells, particularly bivalves, on the surface of which growth rings are often clearly demarcated radiating out from the umbones. These rings are not necessarily seasonal.

In many gastropods, such as the strombs and cowries, the shell changes shape as it matures and often the adult looks nothing like any of its juvenile stages. Most molluscs grow in a regular, orderly fashion so that shells of the same species are similar in shape. Others, such as the worm shells (page 98), grow in an irregular, undisciplined manner so that no two specimens of the same species have the same shape. Some shells are so tiny that it is difficult to understand how

anything can live within them. Others are so large and heavy that it is equally difficult to understand how a soft-bodied animal can be so encumbered and yet survive and propagate.

Easily the largest known shell is that of the Giant Clam of tropical reefs which grows to a length of 1·5 m or more and may weigh well over 225 kg. The largest gastropod is the False Trumpet, from tropical waters in the Pacific, which can be over 50 cm in length. Most shells are nowhere near the size of these giants. The larger squids, of course, leave all the shelled molluscs way behind in the matter of size.

A pin compared with the shell of *Barleeia chasteri* Melvill & Standen; 0·2 cm; Loyalty Is. Many shells are smaller than this. *(opposite page)*

A False Trumpet, *Syrinx aruana* L., used as a water-carrier by a native of NW Australia. This is the largest gastropod shell in the world.

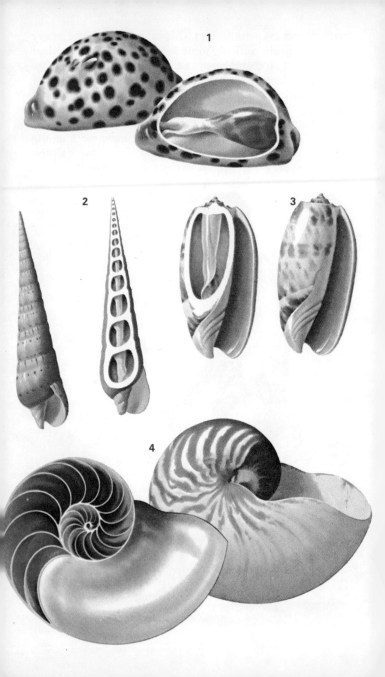

Shell shape

The bewildering variety of shell shape in molluscs is based on the exploitation of a few simple forms. Four of the six molluscan classes have one-piece shells: Monoplacophora, Scaphopoda, Cephalopoda, Gastropoda. It is in these classes, particularly in the last, that the more striking variations of shell shape are found. Most gastropod shells are twisted around an imaginary central axis, and this twisting, or coiling, opens up a wide range of possible shapes that those shells may assume. Starting with a simple tube – such as that which all the tusk shells, but very few gastropods, carry around – almost every conceivable variation may be found until one arrives at the tightly coiled and flattened spiral typical of many land and freshwater snails and some marine prosobranchs. Most gastropods increase the size of their shell without altering its shape. Such growth is logarithmic and the growth curve is called a logarithmic spiral. Possibly the most vital conformation ever exploited by living organisms (no other growth curve is so economical or so adaptable), it helps explain the great success of the gastropods compared with other molluscs (cephalopods excepted). The shell, it should be realized, curves the animal and not the animal the shell: there are innumerable molluscs living in spiral shells, but not one shell-less mollusc is spiral in shape.

Very few cephalopods have coiled shells but some of those that have provide exquisite examples of the logarithmic spiral. The shell of the Pearly Nautilus, when sawn through, is probably the most elegant and certainly the best known example of this type of growth. Because the two valves of bivalve shells are hinged together they cannot exploit anything like the range of shapes that we see in gastropod shells. Some unusual and attractive variations are possible, but sculpture, colour and colour pattern are exploited far more. Chitons vary their overall shape even less than bivalves. Once again it is through variations of sculpture, colour and colour pattern that they express their individuality.

A selection of Indo-Pacific shells in the natural state and sectioned. **1** *Cypraea tigris* L.; 8·8 cm. **2** *Terebra crenulata* L.; 10·0 cm. **3** *Oliva sericea* Röding; 8·2 cm. **4** *Nautilus pompilius* L.; 19·0 cm

Shell sculpture

Completely smooth shells are fairly common and many others have a superficial appearance of glassy smoothness. Cowries and olives have very smooth, porcellaneous shells, but most other shells have at least a few growth lines or other irregularities on the surface. Sculpture (or ornament as it is often called nowadays) may be scarcely perceptible to the naked eye, or so well developed as to mask the basic shell form. Shells of some species of *Latiaxis* and *Murex* are covered in sculpture. The words sculpture and ornament seem inadequate to describe the spines and fins of many shells, but these exaggerated outgrowths really are sculptural and not structural in nature. Most shell sculpture has a balanced, rhythmic appearance because shell growth is a balanced, rhythmic process. Many gastropods have regularly spaced ribs all around the whorls. These indicate rest periods when the mollusc was quiescent long enough to form an apertural lip. Growth continues but the successive false lips remain. Prominent ribs and grooves can be seen on many shells, and though

1 Intricate sculpture shown by *Latiaxis kinoshitai* Fulton; 3·5 cm; Japan. **2** Variation in colour pattern shown by *Palliolum tigerinum* Müller; 2·4 cm; British Is. **3** Variation in colour pattern shown by *Neritina communis* Quoy & Gaimard; 1·6 cm; Philippines

usually parallel to each other they may be at angles, or may cross each other to form a lattice pattern. Instead of, or in addition to, the ribs there may be small protuberances which give a warty appearance. The periostracum of some species may be developed into spines or bristles, but these are easily rubbed off.

Colour pattern

Shape and sculpture alone cannot account for the irresistible attraction of shells. Colour and colour pattern are very important factors too. Many shells are monochromatic (one colour) but most are polychromatic (many colours). Some colours, such as yellow, brown, pink and white – which is really a colour and not an absence of it – are commonly seen, with or without any associated colours. Green, violet and blue are seldom encountered, and no molluscan shell (or any other organic structure) can show true black. Colour banding is common, though shells with more than five bands are rare. Patterns are made up of dots, rectangles, triangles, rings, chevrons, or wavy lines and sometimes they are laid down in an almost mathematically precise way.

2

3

A sandy shore scene

Habitats
Sandy shores
Molluscs which are adapted for burrowing are at home on
sandy shores, and many different kinds of bivalves are
pre-eminently suited to such places. Razor shells and the
shells of *Donax* and *Tellina* may usually be found in plenty:
any limpet found here is likely to be a dead one. A mollusc
which needs to attach itself to a solid object or one which
cannot burrow will not last long on sand.

Rocky shores
Between high and low tide marks on predominantly rocky
shores there is often a varied and abundant molluscan fauna.
Rock pools are happy hunting grounds on almost any shore,
especially in warm waters. With the possible exception of
those found on coral reefs the molluscs of rocky shores

outclass those of other habitats in colour and form. Chitons, limpets, winkles and whelks are adequately sheltered and can find plenty of food without too much effort. Here too rock oysters, mussels and other non-burrowing (or sedentary) bivalves can affix themselves to rocks and other solid objects even though they may sometimes be left high and dry by the receding tide. Some bivalves even bore into the rock and live out their lives in the dark tunnels so created. A mollusc in a warm, clean rock pool has all the essentials and some of the luxuries of life.

Mangrove swamps

In tropical regions mangrove swamps may be formed where the muddy waters discharged by rivers meet up with tidal flats alternately covered and uncovered by the sea. Repellent to most humans the mangrove swamp is a haven for many interesting molluscs, some of which live only in places bathed

A rocky shore scene

by brackish water. Strange-looking oysters cement themselves to the mangrove roots and other bivalves fasten themselves to the same roots with their byssus. Winkles and limpets glide about on the roots inches above the ooze which would suffocate them were they to fall in it. Where sand begins to take over from mud we find a profusion of snails which do not live in the swamp mud or in purer situations. Swamp snails are often notoriously difficult to identify because they are so variable.

Coral reefs

Anyone who can collect in the vicinity of coral reefs is lucky indeed, for many of the world's most beautiful shells are found here and often nowhere else. Cowries and cones are frequently uncovered when a coral head is overturned, and many bivalves lie hidden in the sand or imbedded in the coral rock. Giant clams wedge themselves firmly into the coral and display the brilliant colours of their mantles or

A mangrove swamp scene

A coral reef scene

remain tightly closed. Unfortunately there is money to be made out of coral (although shells are more rewarding commercially) and large tracts of reef are being destroyed by dynamite and other means. Coral reefs, which are formed by animal organisms and not by plant growth as some believe, are easily destroyed but are impossible to replace.

Geographical distribution

That marine molluscs are not distributed haphazardly over the globe is well illustrated by those species which live on the continental shelves (i.e. down to a depth of about 460 m). The fauna of, say, the west coast of Ireland has little in common with that of the east coast of Australia, but it is not very different from that of Newfoundland. Water temperature is one of the factors at work here, the warm waters of the tropical Pacific giving rise to a richer, more colourful fauna than the predominantly cold waters of the Atlantic.

Arctic

Patagonian

West African

Caribbean

Californian

Panamic

Mediterranean

Magellanic

Marine zoogeographical provinces of the world

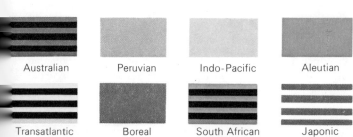

Australian

Peruvian

Indo-Pacific

Aleutian

Transatlantic

Boreal

South African

Japonic

Arctic, Boreal, Mediterranean, Aleutian and Japonic Provinces

Many provinces (or regions) have been proposed but we shall adopt those proposed in the middle of the last century by the Englishman S. P. Woodward, with some minor modifications. At least fifty per cent of the species in each Woodwardian province has to be peculiar to that province. The map shows only the principal ones and some of these are not clearly defined as many species migrate into adjoining provinces. Many species cannot be assigned to any province: all those living below 1830 m, many of those below 460 m, all pelagic species, and some shallow water ones which may drift long distances in their larval stages and so colonize any habitat where they find conditions favourable.

Arctic Province All above the Arctic Circle, east coast of Kamchatka, southern end of Greenland, and east coast of Canada down to the Gulf of St Lawrence. Species relatively few and a high proportion are also found in the Boreal Province. Colourful shells almost unknown. Whelks common but fauna is typified, perhaps, by the gastropods *Margarites* and *Lacuna* and the bivalves *Yoldia* and *Astarte*.

Californian, Panamic and Peruvian Provinces

Boreal Province South coast of Iceland, Norway, Shetlands, Faroes, British Isles, Baltic, North America from the Gulf of St Lawrence to Cape Cod. Many species on North American coast also on coasts of northern Europe. Whelks, winkles, cockles and mussels are characteristic.

Mediterranean (or Lusitanian) Province Mediterranean, Black Sea, Madeira, Azores, Canaries, and from the north-west coast of Africa to the Bay of Biscay. Colourful shells begin to predominate. Numerous genera such as *Columbella*, *Cymbium* and *Cassis* here make their first appearance.

Aleutian Province Coasts of Alaska to British Columbia, Aleutian Islands, Sea of Okhotsk. Mostly sombre species but some are large. *Amicula stelleri*, world's largest chiton, lives here.

Japonic Province Islands of central Japan and east coast of Korea. A no-man's-land between the Boreal and Indo-Pacific Provinces, its temperate waters are ideal for the development of a distinctive and rich fauna. It includes many cones, cowries, volutes and buccinids, besides several slit shells.

33

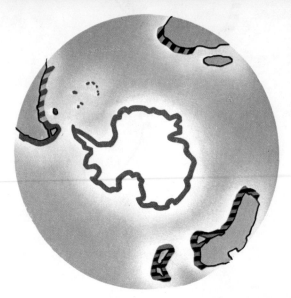

Patagonian, Magellanic, South African and Australian Provinces

Californian Province West coast of the United States of America. A mainly cold-water province containing large abalones and cockles, many limpets and a varied range of chitons.

Panamic (or Panamanian) Province Ecuador to the Gulf of California. An extremely rich fauna containing colourful rock shells, cones, cowries and top shells.

Peruvian Province Similar in many ways to the Panamic Province this contains an equally rich fauna.

Patagonian Province Uruguay and Argentina. Rare volutes and other interesting species mostly found in the depths. Many olives and countless bivalves in shallower waters.

Magellanic Province Tierra del Fuego, Antarctica, South Georgia and other islands in the Southern Ocean. A cold-water area where colourful shells are scarce. Giant sea-weeds cover the rocks and give protection to molluscs. Mussels are everywhere. *Trophon geversianum* is one of the outstanding species.

South African Province South Africa. Fauna greatly influenced by water currents and varied temperatures. More than 800 species recorded from a 16 km stretch of beach at Port Alfred. Rare cowries, slit shells and the world's largest *Marginella* inhabit deep water off Natal.

Australian Province Southern Australia below a line from Brisbane on the east to Geraldton on the west, Tasmania, New Zealand. Though a cool-water province it has many beautiful shells including large volutes and handsome cowries. *Phasianella australis* is the best known of the collectors' favourites.

Transatlantic Province East coast of the United States of America from Cape Cod to half-way down the east coast of Florida. A puzzling mixture of species has led to the establishment of three or four sub-provinces. The Long-necked Clam *(Mya arenaria)* is abundant throughout the province.

Caribbean Province From the southern half of Florida to Rio de Janeiro and encompassing the Antilles. Abounds in truly tropical shells. A collector's paradise offering cowries, cones, olives and helmet shells. *Strombus gigas* is the best-known species.

West African Province From the Cape Verde Islands to the southern end of Angola. Seldom visited by collectors this province has unusual cones and cowries, a single harp shell and large volutes. Characterized by its numerous *Marginella*

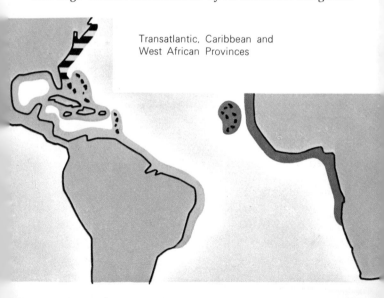

Transatlantic, Caribbean and West African Provinces

species which, collectively, are unequalled elsewhere for beauty.

Indo-Pacific Province Easily the largest province as it comprises the Indian Ocean and most of the Pacific Ocean. Included in it are the island groups of Polynesia and Melanesia, the Indonesian Archipelago, the Hawaiian Chain, Easter Island, Clipperton Island, the northern half of Australia and the southern half of Japan. The coasts bordering the Indian Ocean from Durban round to Singapore, and the coast of Asia bordering the China Sea from Malaya to Korea are also included.

The warm, food-laden waters of this great province (which has defied all attempts to subdivide it) provide conditions ideal for the development of varied molluscan communities. Nowhere else are molluscs so colourful and so numerous. Cowries, cones, volutes, strombs, mitres, terebrids, harps, top shells, olives, murices are all at home here, as well as scallops, rock oysters and giant clams. Sometimes a limited area may

harbour prodigious numbers of a particular species. Around
some of the Maldive Islands in the Indian Ocean certain cowries
are collected constantly and large mounds of them may be
seen at any time, each mound containing millions of shells –
yet the supply seems as inexhaustible as ever. Some bivalves
are equally abundant in some places. Off the Madras and
Bombay coasts of India and around Manila Bay in the Philippines, millions of ark shells are collected and eaten each year.
A patch of only 830 acres in Japan produces 100,000 bushels
of ark shells annually. In Aden ark shells belonging to two
species are raked up into huge mounds to be burnt for lime
(used to whitewash houses). The number of specimens destroyed annually there must be incalculable, but those that
escape give birth to an even greater number. It is no coinci-
dence that most of the illustrations in this book are of Indo-
Pacific seashells; this province has a superabundance of
everything molluscan. There is only one drawback to collecting here: you will never want to collect anywhere else.

Collecting
When to collect
Consult local tide tables to see when the tide is lowest (low spring tide is the ideal time). Collecting is most profitable about an hour after low tide (which may last only twenty minutes) and it is a good plan to work from the lowest point upwards. At night torchlight collecting can be extremely rewarding as molluscs are nocturnal creatures. After storms some beaches are littered with shells many of which live in deeper off-shore waters.

Tools
Do not take more tools than necessary. Much elaborate equipment has only limited application. On the other hand it is useless to hunt for rock-boring molluscs without at least a hammer and chisel, and to dig deep-burrowing bivalves out of wet sand a garden spade is recommended. A metal bar is needed if you want to break open coral blocks, and a short-handled rake is useful if you are hunting for shells in mud. A stout walking stick is useful for turning over rocks and for supporting yourself in rough water; the handle end can be used to drag sea-weed towards you. A scoop of rust-proof metal is useful for sifting sand for the smaller species. A water-glass, which is a box-like device with a glass bottom, enables you to see the sea floor clearly from the surface (a diving mask placed on the water is a serviceable substitute). A light canvas bag may be carried over the shoulder or at the waist to receive larger shells. Plastic bags and polythene tubes, rust-proof forceps, a hand lens (x 10) and a knife are useful additional items. Canvas shoes are indispensable.

Cleaning
Empty shells may need no more than a rinse in warm water and a light brushing. Live-collected specimens are plunged into warm water in a seive and boiled up for two or three minutes (or longer, according to size). The animals can then be removed with a pin or other sharp instrument (bivalves gape on being boiled and the animal can be cut away with a knife). Collectors in the tropics bury partially-cleaned shells in sand and let ants finish the job.

rake

forceps

hook

polythene
collecting tube

hand-lens

specimen bag

scoop

39

Storing specimens

If you want to preserve a mollusc entire it must be kept in a suitable preservative, such as seventy per cent alcohol. Drown the mollusc overnight (in freshwater which has been boiled and cooled previously) and transfer to alcohol next day. Dry shells may be stored in glass tubes of various sizes (stoppered loosely with cotton wool, not corked), match boxes, plastic boxes, and similar containers. Shells placed on coloured foam rubber in clear plastic boxes look very attractive. A simple cabinet consisting of a series of interchangeable hardboard shelves may be constructed very easily.

Labelling specimens

If a collection of shells is to have any lasting value beyond the visual pleasure it gives then the shells must be labelled. The name of the specimen is relatively unimportant because it can be applied at any time subsequent to its discovery. Locality, date of collection, habitat details and similar information intimately associated with it at the time it is collected should be noted immediately. Use pencil for recording notes in the field; use good-quality paper and waterproof black ink for permanent labels.

Naming shells

Without a name for a shell you cannot place it in the collection and it is difficult to find out anything about it. Popular (or vernacular) names are preferred by many persons as being easier to remember. Scientific names are better (most of the popular names are translations of these anyway). The Golden Cowry is the popular name of a large, much-prized shell; its scientific name is *Cypraea aurantium* (the name given to it by J. F. Gmelin in a publication of 1791). The scientific name is understood throughout the world to mean one species and no other; the name Golden Cowry may mean nothing at all to a conchologist in a country where English is unfamiliar. The first part of this name – *Cypraea* – is the genus name (generic name): many molluscan species belong in this genus. The second part – *aurantium* – is the species name (specific name). Only one kind of creature in the animal kingdom bears the name *Cypraea aurantium*.

Cabinet **(1)** and display boxes **(2)**. Hardboard side and back panels slot into a ready-chanelled framework **(3)**. This joint and all others are glued and if possible panel pinned. The drawer frame must be pinned to the hardboard base **(4)**. Finally, the top is glued on and screws are sunk into the frame legs after drilling.

SEASHELLS OF THE WORLD

Scaphopods

These are not the most glamorous of molluscs and their tubular shells are monotonously alike. Some *(Cadulus)* resemble minute, colourless cucumbers, but most are tusk-shaped and have a small slit at the narrower, posterior end. Very few are conspicuously coloured, and as the shells vary only in size, degree of curvature, thickness, position of slit, and similar ill-defined characters their identification is difficult. A species from the north-west coast of North America was once used as currency by the natives, otherwise man has found little use for them. Only some of the larger ones appeal to collectors.

Chitons

Rocks are as essential to chitons as they are to limpets and abalones. Consequently

1 *Pictodentalium formosum* Adams & Reeve; 4·7 cm; W Pacific. 2 *Dentalium elephantinum* L.; 8·0 cm; Indo-Pacific Prov. 3 *Acanthochitona exquisita* Pilsbry; 3·2 cm; Gulf of California. 4 *Loricella angasi* H. Adams; 3·5 cm; S Australia. 5 *Tonicia elegans* Frembly; 4·4 cm; Peruvian Prov

sandy shores are devoid of chitons while the rocky coast of Chile is famous for them. The largest species is the 25 cm *Amicula stelleri* Middendorff, a well-known intertidal animal found off the coasts of Alaska and northern California. The majority of species are much smaller than this and a few are minute by comparison. The shelly plates vary in shape and disposition in the various genera, some species resembling armour-plated slugs while others have the plates so reduced and embedded in the animal's fleshy back that they provide scarcely any protection. Apart from the variations in ornament and colour exhibited by the valves there is much variation in the composition and colour of the encircling leathery girdle. It may be smooth and dull coloured, or decorated with spines, tufts of bristles or granulations, or it may be more colourful than the valves. Chitons normally have eight valves but abnormal forms with six, seven or nine valves have been found. To prepare these creatures for the collection they must be tied down to a flat piece of wood so that they die without curling up.

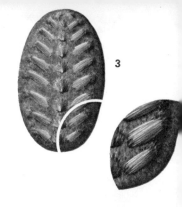

3

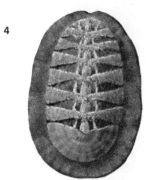

4

5

Cephalopods

Most of us seldom see living cephalopods except captive ones. In some parts of the world, however, they are abundant, and squids 3·7 m long, weighing anything up to 160 kg, swarm in the Humboldt Current off Peru. They are so rapacious there that it is almost impossible to fish one out of the water before it is eaten by its fellows (easy prey for creatures which can chop wooden poles to pieces or bite through strong steel wire with their beaks). A human being would be devoured

Paper Nautilus, *Argonauta argo* L.; 16·0 cm; almost world-wide in warm seas. The egg case resembles a real shell and is astonishingly light and fragile.

in seconds. Few cephalopods (and no other invertebrates) are as fearsome as the Humboldt Current squids and most are small and harmless. The octopus is shell-less and so of little interest to collectors, and the squid has merely a horn-like internal shell (called a 'pen' because it resembles the quill-pen which used to be fashioned out of a bird's feather). The cuttle-fish also has an internal shell, known as a cuttle-bone (familiar as the white substance given to cage-birds) and this gives rigidity to the body. *Spirula* has a small coiled shell which is also internally situated, and this is sometimes washed up on beaches. True external shells are found only in the few species of *Nautilus*. An inspiration to mathematicians, poets and painters, the shell of the Pearly Nautilus is one of Nature's

Nautilus scrobiculatus Lightfoot; 12·5 cm; Pacific

best-known 'cast-offs'. Sectioned, it is seen to have a chambered construction (page 23), the compartments having once been filled with a gas or a fluid, the quantities of which the shell's occupant could vary to allow it to ascend or descend in the water at will. *N. scrobiculatus* is a rare species coveted by collectors. The Paper Nautilus is a very different creature to the Pearly Nautilus. We have already seen that its shell is really an egg-case (although not less prized by collectors on that account). A female argonaut may be 30 cm or more in length and the male about a centimetre.

1 *Acila fultoni* Smith; 3·1 cm; Indian Ocean. **2** *Nucula tenuis* Montagu; 0·9 cm; Boreal Prov. **3** *Solemya solen* von Salis; 2·4 cm; Mediterranean Prov. **4** *Limopsis grandis* Smith; 2·8 cm; Magellanic Prov. **5** *Trisidos tortuosa* L.; 9·5 cm; Indo-Pacific Prov

Bivalves
Awning clams (Solemyacea)
The most primitive of all bivalves are probably the awning clams. Their shells are extremely thin and fragile and the dark brown periostracum extends well beyond the edges of the valves. Unlike all other bivalves they burrow into the sand or other substrate rear end first. By closing the shell valves and expelling water from the siphonal end, at the same time expanding and withdrawing the foot, an awning clam can make leaping or darting movements, as many as 90 to 100 per minute in some species.

Nut clams (Nuculacea)
Nut clams are not attractive externally but they have lustrous pearly interiors which were used by Victorian ladies in many of their shell-work creations. In the genus *Acila* the shells are ornamented externally with chevron-like grooves and ridges by which they are easily distinguished from their mostly smooth-shelled cousins. Few nut clams live in shallow water. Conversely, they comprise the numerically largest group of abyssal bivalves.

Ark shells (Arcacea)
When opened the ark shells are conspicuous for their numerous interlocking hinge teeth arranged in straight lines. Many species fasten themselves to solid objects by a byssus, and there is sometimes a gaping (byssal) notch through which it is extruded. *Arca senilis* L., an extremely thick-shelled species, is eaten by natives along the West African coast. *A. granosa* L. is also eaten in many parts of the world, although it does not live up to the gastronomic promise suggested by its red flesh. *Trisidos tortuosa* is remarkable for its odd shape which gives the impression of a straight-sided shell having been held in someone's two hands and the ends twisted in contrary directions.

Bittersweets (Limopsacea)
The hairy periostracum of the bittersweet clams and their relatives differs strikingly from that of the awning clams. Some species of *Glycymeris* may be thickly covered with an

almost downy periostracum that completely hides the shell underneath. *Limopsis grandis* is more thinly covered but the periostracal hairs are relatively longer and coarser.

Mussels (Mytilacea)

Nearly all mussels are elongated and are broadest at the posterior end. The Edible Mussel of European waters typifies the group which is esteemed the world over as a nutritious food. The Green Mussel is an Indian Ocean species eaten in many places around the coast of India, particularly when fish is scarce and costly. Its vivid green exterior contrasts strikingly with the blue or brown colour of its European counterpart. *Choromytilus chorus*, which is commonly used for food in Chile, is a giant among mussels and may grow up to 18 cm in length. Horse mussels have somewhat rectangular shells which may be smooth or covered with a densely hairy periostracum.

1

1 *Choromytilus chorus* Molina, natural and polished; 15·0 cm; Peruvian and Patagonian Provs. **2** *Malleus malleus* L.; 19·0 cm; Indo-Pacific Prov. **3** *Modiolus hanleyi* Dunker; 9·0 cm; Japan. **4** Green Mussel, *Mytilus viridis* L.; 5·5 cm; Indian Ocean

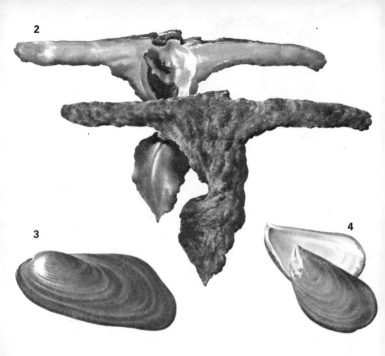

2

3

4

Like the edible mussels the interiors of their shells are lustrous and sometimes iridescent. Some of them are edible too, but in places they are unwanted pests. The Gulf of Manaar, separating Ceylon and southern India, is a rich breeding ground for pearl oysters, but these commercially desirable creatures find that they have to share their floor space with other molluscs. Horse mussels are particularly abundant here and several square miles of sea bottom may be covered by a thick carpet of them all tangled together in their own byssal threads. The delicate pearl oyster larvae stand no chance of survival in such a place. Date mussels, resembling smooth cigars, spend their adult life boring into rocks, corals or shells, and the only effective way to collect them is to break open their homes with a steel bar. That such fragile creatures can burrow into such durable materials seemed incredible until it was discovered that they secrete an acid which softens calcareous substances.

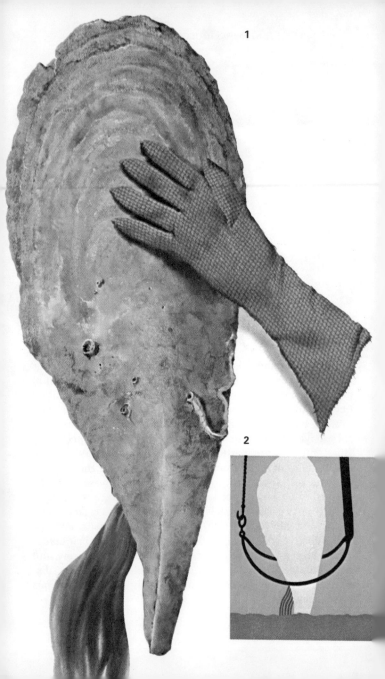

1

2

Pearl oysters and wing mussels (Pteriacea)

In their life history and habits the pearl oysters resemble the mussels. In some places they occur in prodigious quantities; in 1905 over eighty million specimens of *Pinctada radiata* were fished up at the Ceylon pearl fishery in six weeks! Renowned for the pearls they produce, the shells themselves are valuable also as a source of mother-of-pearl. But the all-conquering plastics industry has reduced the demand for pearl shell. Wing mussels differ from pearl oysters by the long 'ears' or 'wings' they develop on either side of the umbones.

Pen shells (Pteriacea)

The shells of these large bivalves are thin and fragile which is probably why man has found little use for them. On the other hand he has been able to utilize the byssus of at least one species in an unexpected way. The Noble Pen Shell, the largest of all pen shells, spins a fine, silky byssus which, after being processed, can be made into high-quality garments and smaller items of an ornamental nature. Before the universal diffusion of silk there was an important 'byssus industry' centred on Taranto in southern Italy. The garments made from byssus thread are durable and attractive, but as each mollusc produces only a single gram of byssus the industry is unlikely to flourish again.

3   **4**

1 Noble Pen Shell, *Pinna nobilis* L.; 40·0 cm; Mediterranean Prov. Glove is made from its byssus. **2** Method of fishing for Noble Pen Shell. **3** *Pteria peasei* Dunker; 9·5 cm; Indo-Pacific Prov. **4** *Pinctada radiata* Leach; 6·5 cm; Indo-Pacific Prov

File shells (Limacea)

Some molluscan animals are more attractive than the shells they live in, and this is certainly true of the file shells. Off-white or yellow in colour and usually rough in texture (hence their popular name), they exhibit little difference from species to species except in size. But the tenants of these shells atone for their drab exteriors by displaying long, colourful tentacles all around the edges of the shell valves, particularly when swimming. At such times these molluscs become an

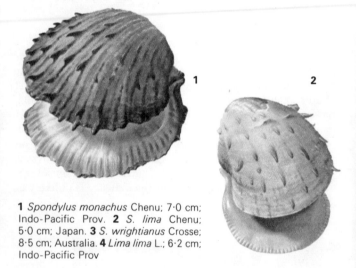

1 *Spondylus monachus* Chenu; 7·0 cm; Indo-Pacific Prov. **2** *S. lima* Chenu; 5·0 cm; Japan. **3** *S. wrightianus* Crosse; 8·5 cm; Australia. **4** *Lima lima* L.; 6·2 cm; Indo-Pacific Prov

unforgettably beautiful sight.

For most of their lives, however, they conceal themselves in nests which they construct from broken shells and other debris held together by byssal threads and mucus.

Thorny oysters (Pectinacea)

Thorny oysters are among the few bivalve groups favoured by collectors – and no wonder. With their long spines and bright colours they are an arresting sight in a collector's cabinet. As they cement themselves to rocks sometimes as much as 30 m below the surface and are usually covered with algae, sponges and coral growths they are not so arresting in their native haunts.

Cleaning a thorny oyster can be a long and frustrating task, but the end product is well worth the trouble. The quieter the water the longer the spines tend to grow, though some species have poorly developed spines no matter where they live. The lower, cemented valve is usually cup-shaped and the upper, flatter one is, perhaps obviously, the more spiny and more colourful. Sediment can be prevented from settling in

the lower valve even though the shell is permanently fixed; the upper valve can be rapidly flapped up and down so that the sediment is expelled as it alights on the mantle edge.

Although known popularly as thorny oysters they are not related to oysters at all but to scallops. Superficially they resemble some of the jewel boxes *(Chama*, page 62) but the structure of the animals as well as the inner construction of the shells shows that the two groups are totally unrelated. There are many so-called species of thorny oysters living in the warmer waters of the world but because they are so variable in size, shape, ornamentation and colour it is more than probable that scientists have named and described many more species than actually exist.

Scallops (Pectinacea)

It is a matter of opinion which is the best painting of Venus but the most famous is probably that by Botticelli: significantly his Venus stands on a floating scallop valve. Close relatives of the thorny oysters and much more widespread over the globe, scallops have always been great favourites with men and women and not only those with artistic tendencies. The delicious taste of the cooked animal is the scallop's principal attraction now, but until fairly recently the shell was coveted too, and sometimes it was revered. As a symbol the shell was the basis of motifs utilized in the manufacture of mosaics, pottery, coins, statuary and other Roman artifacts, and the earliest recorded examples of such motifs are well over 2,000 years old.

Perhaps the best known scallop is the Great Scallop (*Pecten maximus* L.). It is, arguably, the tastiest of all edible molluscs, and it is now familiar to millions as the trade symbol of the Shell Oil Group. It may be the most familiar scallop but it is not the most beautiful, many tropical species being brilliantly coloured. *Gloripallium pallium*, for instance, puts it to shame.

Some scallops, like file shells, can swim, and they quickly do so should a starfish or other predator approach them. By opening and rapidly closing their valves they can move in almost any direction by a kind of jet propulsion. Not all scallops can swim and some are attached by a byssus to other objects throughout their lives.

Another interesting feature of some of these animals can be seen around the mantle edge of each valve. At intervals there are diamond-like eyes, up to a hundred in some species, each eye possessing a lens, a retina and an optic nerve. Exactly how these organs function is not known for certain but they are definitely sensitive to light, and the valves close immediately if the shadow of an object falls across the eyes.

1 *Gloripallium pallium* L.; 6·6 cm; Indo-Pacific Prov. **2** *Chlamys sanguinolentus* Gmelin; 5·5 cm; Red Sea. **3** *C. varia* L.; 4·4 cm; Boreal Prov

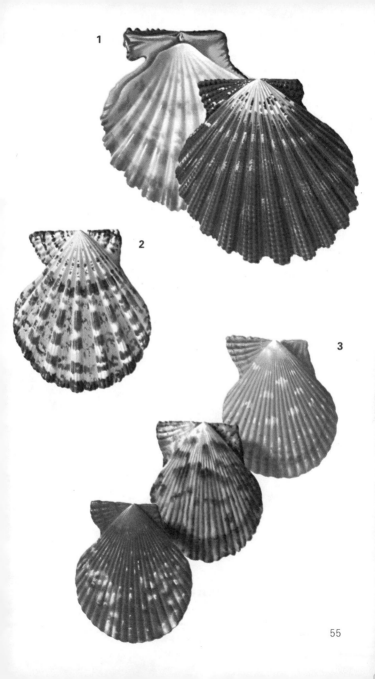

Windowpane oysters (Pectinacea)

Windowpane oysters have no byssus and lie freely on their concave left valves, usually on muddy bottoms of estuaries and land-locked bays, and often they occur in millions. Man has found a commercial use for such shells, especially for the small ones which are usually clear, translucent and colourless. It was discovered long ago that they were excellent for glazing windows and verandah roofs. In the Philippines they are still fished up in large numbers and manufactured into screens, windows, lamp shades and ornaments.

Jingle shells (Anomiacea)

Allied to the scallops and other byssus-attached molluscs the jingle shells differ markedly in the nature of their byssal attachment. The byssal threads are fused together into a thick stalk which protrudes through a hole in the middle of the lower valve and is fixed to the substrate. The upper valve,

1 Windowpane Oyster, *Placuna placenta* L.; 13·0 cm; Indo-Pacific Prov. **2** Lamp made in Philippines from shells of Windowpane Oyster. **3** Cock's-comb Oyster, *Lopha cristagalli* L.; 15·0 cm (the whole clump); Indo-Pacific Prov

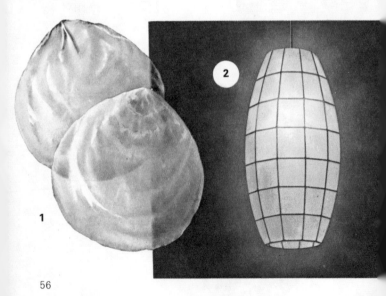

3

which fits over the animal rather like a limpet shell, often resembles the surface on which the lower valve lies. *Enigmonia aenigmatica* Holten, from northern Australia, is remarkable for its ability to crawl – a singular adaptation for a mollusc whose closest relatives spend their lives in enforced immobility – and often crawls up foliage above water level.

Oysters (Ostreacea)

As staple items of food in many countries, oysters are among the best known of all molluscs, and prodigious quantities are eaten annually. At the end of the nineteenth century about forty million oysters were being sold each year in Britain alone! There are many different oyster species, most of them edible, and several have curiously indented edges to the valves which enhance their otherwise dull appearance. These are more difficult to open than the smooth-edged kinds and so are less likely to end up on a dinner table. Although an oyster may lay up to fifty million eggs in a spawning season perhaps only a dozen will reach the adult stage. In the entire animal kingdom there can be few creatures with such a high infant mortality rate.

Brooch shells (Trigoniacea)

These are among the most attractive of bivalves chiefly because of their delicately tinted and nacreous interiors. Their exteriors, by contrast, are various shades of brown and are strongly ribbed. As they are common in some places (though unknown in the living state outside Australian and Tasmanian waters) they are made into spoons, brooches and similar fancy goods. Comparable shells are found as fossils in deposits of great age throughout the world but none were known to be still living until early in the nineteenth century when Samuel Stutchbury, a competent conchologist, dredged one up in Sydney Harbour. Unfortunately this specimen leapt back into the sea! (It is now well known that some brooch shells can leap several centimetres by means of their angular and muscular foot). Luckily Stutchbury obtained another one three months later.

Astartes and crassatellas (Crassatellacea)

With their dull brown coloration and simple outline the typically cold-water-loving astartes are not very attractive. Crassatellas are not very attractive either, but some of them are certainly built to last. One South Australian species is so strongly constructed and has such sharp-edged valves that it has been used as a hand axe by natives there. *Eucrassatella kingicola*, a related species, is just as solidly built.

Carditas (Carditacea)

Many of the widespread carditas are colourful and some have scaly shells. *Thecalia* is peculiar for the brood chamber, formed on the inner surface of the valves.

The Heart Cockle (Glossacea)

The Heart Cockle, which is not a cockle at all, is remarkable for the almost snail-like coiling of the umbones.

1 Heart Cockle, *Glossus humanus* L.; 7·0 cm; Boreal-Mediterranean Provs. **2** *Astarte sulcata* da Costa; 2·7 cm; Boreal-Mediterranean Provs. **3** *Cardita umbonata* Sowerby; 3·5 cm; W African Prov. **4** *Neotrigonia margaritacea* Lamarck; 4·5 cm; S Australia. **5** *Eucrassatella kingicola* Lamarck; 5·5 cm; S Australia. **6** *Thecalia concamerata* Bruguière; 1·3 cm; Indo-Pacific Prov

The Iceland Cyprina (Arcticacea)

A common species in the North Atlantic the Iceland Cyprina is large and thick shelled, and the periostracum covering it is also thick. If a live specimen is collected and killed by pouring boiling water on it be prepared for a shock and then a disappointment. A loud report, resembling a gun shot, provides the shock; and disappointment soon follows when it is realized that the shell valves are cracked or shattered. The disastrous effects of boiling water may be due to a peculiarity in the shell's structure.

Coral clams (Arcticacea)

The burrows of other rock-boring molluscs provide ready-made homes for coral clams. The shells of some coral clams bear a striking resemblance to those of date mussels, which are true rock borers, but there are hinge teeth in the clams and not in the mussels.

Myllitas, leptons and Vasconiella (Leptonacea)

These groups include some of the world's tiniest bivalves as well as some of the more bizarre. The exquisite sculpture

1 *Trapezium oblongum* L.; 5·0 cm; Indian Ocean. 2 *Coralliophaga coralliophaga* Gmelin; 4·0 cm; Indian Ocean. 3 *Vasconiella jeffreysiana* Fischer; 0·6 cm; Bay of Biscay. 4 Shrimp's Burrow Lepton, *Ephippodonta macdougalli* Tate; 1·0 cm; S Australia. 5 *Mylitta deshayesi* d'Orbigny & Récluz; 1·3 cm; S Australia. 6 Iceland Cyprina, *Arctica islandica* L.; 8·0 cm; Boreal-Mediterranean Provs

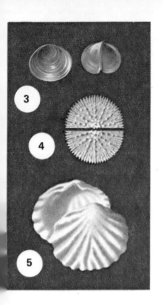

on the myllitas is best seen with a hand lens or microscope as some of the species have shells only 2 mm long. They are familiar to collectors in Australia and Tasmania where so many of the smaller bivalves are found. The Shrimp's Burrow Lepton, known only from South Australia, is surely among the oddest of all bivalves. It lives in the burrows of a shrimp, creeps about like a snail, and always has its valves open at an angle of at least seventy degrees. The minute hinge teeth in each valve do not interlock and barely touch each other. On the other side of the globe, on a secluded beach in the south-west of France, the translucent valves of *Vasconiella jeffreysiana* can be found washed up at the high-tide mark. They are of unusual interest because some are flat and circular and some are concave and have a deep notch in one side. Described in 1872 on the basis of a single indented (right) valve dredged from deep water off the west coast of France, it was not until 1957 that a complete specimen was found, near St Jean-de-Luz. This showed the dissimilarity between the two valves. Nobody has ever seen the animal occupant of this unique type of bivalve, and its mode of life is unknown.

Lucinas (Lucinacea)

Many of the shells which belong to this group and to the following group (the jewel boxes) are both large and thick, and although some are colourful most are white or whitish. The common Basket Lucina is ornamented with close-set, concentric ridges intersected by strong radial ridges, the overall effect being a kind of basket weave. Its close relative, the Elegant Basket Lucina, has distinct pinkish rays which make it an even more attractive shell; it is also much the rarer and is a collector's item. Both occur in Australian waters and elsewhere in the Pacific. The Red-lipped Codakia is remarkable for the red margin around the inside edge of the valves; the red colour does not appear on the outside of the valves.

1

1 Red-lipped Codakia, *Codakia tigerina* L.; 8·3 cm; Pacific. **2** Elegant Basket Lucina, *Fimbria soverbii* Reeve; 6·0 cm; SW Pacific. **3** *Pseudochama corrugata* Broderip; 5·0 cm; Panamic Prov. **4** Basket Lucina, *Fimbria fimbriata* L.; 5·8 cm; Pacific

Jewel boxes (Chamacea)

The most striking fact about the jewel boxes concerns the mode of attachment of the shell to other objects. This does not seem to differ markedly from that of the thorny oysters, species of each group permanently cementing themselves by one valve to the substrate. It is only when you open the valves that you notice something odd about them. By studying the hinge teeth it becomes obvious that most kinds of jewel boxes are cemented by the left valve and a few others by the right. At one time it was thought that this represented the bivalve equivalent of the phenomenon of abnormal coiling seen in some gastropod shells (page 12). It is now known that most species in this group cement themselves by the left valve and very few by the right valve. There is still no known instance among the bivalves of a specimen having been found in which all the features of the right valve have developed in the left valve, and vice versa. Jewel boxes are all inhabitants of warm seas and abound in coral reef areas. As they grow older they are likely to become heavily encrusted with all kinds of marine growth and therefore young specimens are usually more attractive and more suitable for a collection. Superb shells of mature growth may sometimes be collected from flat-sided, artificial structures, such as sunken concrete slabs.

Cockles (Cardiacea)

It may come as a surprise to learn that the world's largest bivalve, the Giant Clam, is second cousin to the common European Cockle; and that a human being could consume a plateful of the latter while sitting comfortably in one valve of the former. Even among the true cockles there is great diversity in size, shape and colour. The European Cockle is

1 *Ctenocardia victor* Angas; 3·6 cm; Indian Ocean. **2** European Cockle; 4·2 cm (shell only); Boreal Prov. **3** Belcher's Cockle, *Trachycardium belcheri* Broderip & Sowerby; 4·3 cm; Panamic Prov. **4** *Corculum cardissa* L.; 6·1 cm; Indo-Pacific Prov

certainly one of the least inspiring to look at, especially when compared with some tropical cockles such as *Ctenocardia victor* and Belcher's Cockle. The sculpture and colour of the shell of Belcher's Cockle must surely be among the most exquisite in the whole shell world. The heart cockles *(Corculum)* comprise another extremely attractive group which bear little resemblance to those shells whose sandy occupants some of us actually enjoy eating.

Let us conclude our discussion of the cockles with a few facts about cockles in Britain, a part of the world in which it is prudent to be born anything but a mollusc, especially an edible one. The European Cockle is abundant in some places here, as many as 10,000 having been recorded in one square metre. In the Wash and Thames Estuary the daily catch of

cockles per man may exceed 610 kg, and there is no apparent end to the supply. In the Burry Inlet region of South Wales the discarded shells form extensive mounds which never seem to diminish no matter how many are sold for crushing to make poultry grit. They are preyed upon to an enormous extent by birds, fishes, starfish and by other molluscs. Whole beds of them may be wiped out by severe frost or by encroachment of sand. Those that survive this far have the likely prospect of being raked up, bundled into sacks, boiled or steamed alive, stripped of their shells, sold and eaten. Approximately 1,778,100 kg of them end up this way each year in Britain.

Giant clams (Tridacnacea)

Six species are included in the family Tridacnidae, only one of which, *Tridacna gigas*, should be referred to as *the* Giant Clam. With the exception of the Bear's Paw, however, each of the others is commonly regarded as *a* giant clam. *T. gigas* is the largest living bivalve known, and few invertebrates are larger, fewer still being heavier. The largest pair of valves recorded measured 135 cm in length. The heaviest on record, now in the American Museum of Natural History, New York, weighs 263 kg, and several others are known which exceed 225 kg. All giant clams are restricted to the Indo-Pacific faunal region and flourish best where the water is warmest. Such massive creatures are hardly likely to attain maximum size overnight, and though there is no agreement over the duration of their life-span (estimates varying from eight years to several hundred years), it seems that they are long lived under natural conditions. Experimental evidence indicates that they add approximately 5 cm to the shell in the course of a year.

A remarkable feature of giant clams is their association with large numbers of algae, called zooxanthellae, which they 'farm' within that part of the mantle which is exposed when the mollusc (which is permanently anchored in the adult stage) is covered by water. The zooxanthellae flourish there, and ultimately they reach the digestive gland and are digested. It is probable that zooxanthellae comprise the principal food of these large creatures. Sizeable pearls, usually worthless, have been collected from giant clams. The 'Pearl of Allah', weighing 7 kg and measuring 24 cm by 14 cm, is the largest and heaviest of these ever recorded and was on show recently in a Los Angeles jeweller's shop. The clam which formed it is supposed to have killed the diver who found it, and though this was not proved satisfactorily it would seem likely that such massive creatures could retain human limbs fast in their two tightly-closed valves, with fatal consequences. Surprisingly there are hardly any well-authenticated stories of human fatalities caused in this way and it is certain that most of the stories are apocryphal. The growing edges of a giant clam are very sharp, however, and can inflict deep and painful wounds if handled carelessly.

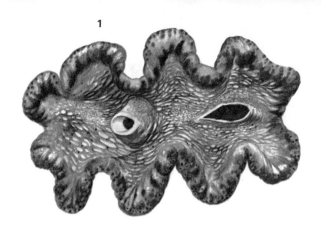

Giant Clam, *Tridacna gigas* L.;
Pacific. **1** Animal as seen from
above, showing siphons and
mantle. **2** Empty shell

Venus clams (Veneracea)

This very extensive group of bivalves is distributed all over the globe and most of the shells are thick and heavy relative to their overall size. Some are beautifully patterned and the variation of pattern within a single species is sometimes remarkable. The striking zig-zag pattern seen on some shells of *Sunetta scripta* may be replaced, in others, by plain rays of dark colour with light interspaces. Obviously the light interspaces and the zig-zags correspond to each other. Nearly all venus clams burrow in sand and are easy to collect. Often they occur in prodigious numbers and may, in places, be important articles of food.

1

1 Northern Quahog, *Mercenaria mercenaria* L.; 8·0 cm; Transatlantic Prov and introduced into Boreal Prov. **2** *Sunetta scripta* L.; 4·0 cm; Indo-Pacific Prov. **3** *Callista erycina* L.; 6·8 cm; Indo-Pacific Prov

Among the better known edible ones is the Northern Quahog which is marketed in the eastern United States. Years ago sea-worn fragments of the heavy, thick shell of this species were perforated and strung on leather thongs by North American Indians ('quahog' – meaning 'tightly closed' – is derived from the name given to it by them). This constituted their 'wampum', a form of coinage used in all their business transactions, and they also utilized it for dress ornamentation. They ate the mollusc too, and it has been preyed upon for food by humans ever since. The human species is not its only natural predator, starfish and boring molluscs being partial to it as well. Birds too seem to esteem it a delicacy. It is now familiar to most Americans in the form of clam chowders and clams-on-the-half-shell. Because of its potential value as a nutritious food several attempts have

2

3

been made to naturalize it around European coasts, but most of the attempts have been unsuccessful. There are now thriving colonies of the Northen Quahog in several places off British, French and Dutch coasts, but most of these established themselves with very little human assistance (though doubtless they were adventitiously introduced by humans in the first place). One day clams-on-the-half-shell may become as familiar to Europeans as they are to Americans. On the other hand the competition provided by native oysters, cockles, scallops and mussels may prove to be too much for them.

Most venus clams burrow into soft sand or silt, but usually they do not burrow very deeply and this is why many of them have stout, thick shells (bivalves which burrow deeply do not need to be so well protected and so most of them are thin-shelled). A large group of bivalves such as this is likely to contain shells which differ very much from each other. Because they do not burrow deeply they can afford the extravagance of exaggerated processes on the shell. The shells shown here indicate something of this variety of form and sculpture. They may be fragile, strong and flattened, frilled, or spiny. The Comb Venus, with its long and elegant spines, is one of several similar species which have always been considered collectors' items (though they are certainly not rare) particularly if their spines are long and intact.

Readers of the 'James Bond' books may recall the heroine of *Dr No* searching the shore of a Caribbean island for a certain kind of shell. It was a species closely related to the Comb Venus that she was after. Ian Fleming was a keen shell collector and wrote several articles on Caribbean seashells before he became famous as Bond's creator. The Comb Venus is one of sixty or more venus clams inhabiting the Panamic Province. Many more species are found in the Indo-Pacific Province, and Australia is a happy hunting ground for them. The dosinias are often found washed up on tidal flats and beaches there. After storms you may be lucky enough to find a Frilled Venus though it is best to use a dredge to get living ones from below low tide mark. When freshly collected the 'frills' are tinted bright pink and the whole shell is then lovely to look at; for obvious reasons it is known also as the Wedding Cake Venus. There is never a sufficient quantity of fine quality specimens of this exquisite species to go round as collectors are always waiting to pounce on them.

1 *Lioconcha castrensis* L.; 4·2 cm; Pacific. **2** Comb Venus, *Hysteroconcha lupanaria* Lesson; 7·7 cm; Panamic Prov. **3** *Circe scripta* L.; 3·8 cm; Indo-Pacific Prov. **4** Frilled Venus, *Bassinadisjecta* Perry; 6·5 cm; S Australia

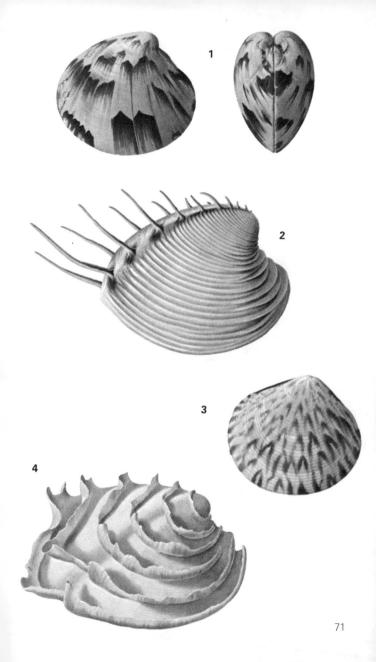

Trough shells and otter shells (Mactracea)

The group to which all these shells belong is easily distinguished from other bivalve groups. Most of the shells have a large internal ligament which is attached to a deep, spoon-shaped cup (or chondrophore) in the middle of the hinge plate. They are well adapted for burrowing, most of them being thin, light and smooth, and several are streamlined in

1 Common Otter Shell, *Lutraria lutraria* L.; 11·0 cm; Boreal-W African and S African Provs. 2 Rayed Trough Shell, *Mactra corallina* L.; 5·2 cm; Boreal Prov. 3 *Scissodesma spengleri* L.; 8·3 cm; S African Prov

appearance. The muscular foot of the Rayed Trough Shell is sometimes used for leaping, an activity which can be observed on placing a specimen in a dish of sea water. At one time shells of this species were used in Holland for making roads and foot-paths, and this indicates how abundant they are in places.

The Common Otter Shell, which is seldom obtained alive except by digging, lives in muddy sand about 60 cm below the surface, but it can eject water out of its burrow to a height of several centimetres.

Some of the trough shells and otter shells are edible and, in fact, they once were staple articles of food in coastal districts of western France, Spain, southern Britain and elsewhere. However, they are among the more unattractive of the edible molluscs and it is doubtful if many persons eat them nowadays. The British recipe for preparing them for the table was simple: boil them, and then eat them with salt and vinegar (a recipe which the British are inclined to use for almost anything edible). A large kind of otter shell used to be an important article of winter food for the Indian tribes living along the coasts of British Columbia and Vancouver Island. As it was considered detrimental to the dignity of the men to dig for them the job was delegated to their squaws who used a bent stick to rake them up. After placing them on red-hot stones to open the shells they removed the animals and threaded them on to hemp cords, smoked them over a fire, and finally strung them up. They were then taken down and eaten by the tribe as required. By comparison the prospect of death by starvation seems almost pleasant.

Wedge shells (Tellinacea)

These, and the closely related tellins, have similar shells, and the animals of each have long siphons as in *Donax trunculus*. Because they live in shallow waters and are constantly hunted for food by sea birds, fish and humans they find it advantageous to live well buried in the sand with the tips of their siphons just level with the surface; if alarmed they withdraw the siphons and burrow down even further. It is significant that the commonest wedge shells appear to be those with the longest siphons. They are among the commonest of all shallow-water bivalves, and as nearly all of them are edible

1

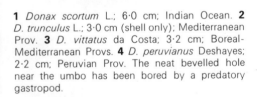

1 *Donax scortum* L.; 6·0 cm; Indian Ocean. **2** *D. trunculus* L.; 3·0 cm (shell only); Mediterranean Prov. **3** *D. vittatus* da Costa; 3·2 cm; Boreal-Mediterranean Provs. **4** *D. peruvianus* Deshayes; 2·2 cm; Peruvian Prov. The neat bevelled hole near the umbo has been bored by a predatory gastropod.

enormous quantities are collected and eaten by humans each year. Like other brightly coloured shells they are more numerous in tropical waters. Most of the species are fairly smooth and glossy but some of them, including *D. scortum* which is one of the larger species, are coarsely sculptured. The valves of *D. scortum* show little variation in colour, but others are so variable that no two valves have similar colouring.

D. peruvianus, one of the more colourful species, is commonly seen for sale in Peruvian markets. It is extremely abundant in Peruvian waters and must have been an important article of food among Peruvian Indians before the arrival of the conquistadores. Thick layers of the bleached valves of *D. peruvianus* are conspicuous features of some of their burial mounds.

Man-made imitations of the valves of *D. vittatus* have been utilized in an interesting experiment to determine how the natural valves of this and other bivalves are transported

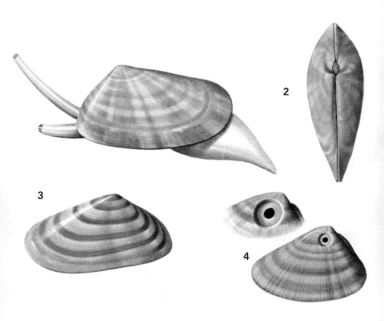

by water currents. At low tide thousands of artificial valves, differing in weight, size and other factors, were laid out in small circles at the lower part of the shore. After the following ebb tide the distribution of valves on the beach was studied. The results showed that the valves had been sorted into different categories. Most noticeable was the way in which right valves ended up clearly separated from left valves. In nature

75

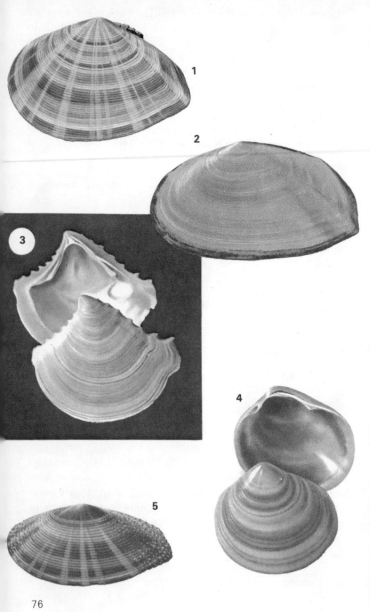

76

this could mean that anyone collecting the valves of a certain bivalve species from the beach should not be surprised if he picked up many more left valves than right valves (or vice versa).

Tellins (Tellinacea)

Compared with the wedge shells, to which they are closely allied, tellins are much more numerous in species and genera and are more colourful. Their valves lack the serrated edges which characterize most wedge shells, and the right and left valves of many tellins are unequal in shape and size. They are found in sand or sandy-mud substrates and few species live in estuarine waters. *Tellina foliacea* is a handsome, smooth-shelled species which often takes on a muddy appearance as it lives in the vicinity of mangrove swamps. *Tellina virgata* is easily recognized by its pink or red colour bands which radiate from the umbones, a colour pattern to which it owes its popular name, Striped Sunset Shell. *Tellidora burneti* cannot be mistaken for any other bivalve (with the exception of a single Caribbean species belonging to the same genus).

In most tellins the surface sculpture is regularly disposed over the valves and either radiates from the umbones or is concentric to them. There are numerous species belonging to several genera, however, in which the sculpture is neither radial nor concentric but wavy (or 'scissulate' as it is now termed). This sculpture is well seen in *Strigilla*. The scissulations are so distinctive and invariable in this genus that they have been employed to subdivide it into several sub-genera. As several genera have evolved this kind of sculpture independently it has been assumed that it reflects a similar way of life, that it has something to do with helping the shell to maintain a certain position in the sand. In one or two species the scissulations are developed on the right valve only. At the present time there is insufficient evidence to show in

1 Striped Sunset Shell, *Tellina virgata* L.; 5·7 cm; Indo-Pacific Prov.
2 *T. foliacea* L.; 7·0 cm; Pacific. **3** *Tellidora burneti* Broderip & Sowerby; 4·3 cm; Panamic Prov. **4** *Strigilla carnaria* L.; 2·6 cm; Caribbean Prov.
5 *Tellina pulcherrima* Sowerby; 4·2 cm; Indo-Pacific Prov

what way, if any, species of *Strigilla* and other genera benefit from this peculiar sculpture.

Razor shells (Solenacea)
In the razor shells we see possibly the most perfect examples of adaptation to a burrowing existence to be found among molluscs. Smooth, narrow, long, and either straight-sided or slightly curved, their shells can be drawn down at a remarkable rate by the animal whose foot is plunged into the sand and made to swell out, so giving it the necessary purchase. Some razor shells are able to move at such a speed that they can burrow down as fast as the collector can dig. Seasoned collectors know that there is an easier way to catch them. If some salt is poured into their holes then sometimes they will jump out.

Soft-shelled clams and others (Myacea)
The soft-shelled clams are not suited to rapid burrowing and if dislodged from their hiding places deep in the sand it is almost impossible for them to get back again. The Long-necked Clam was so named because of its long siphon which is permanently extended, being much too large to be accommodated within the shell. Although the siphon is encased in a tough leathery sheath and the whole mollusc is otherwise unappetizing to look at, there is a demand for it as food and great quantities are fished commercially off the eastern coast of the United States of America. The largest and heaviest bivalved shell to be found in the northern hemisphere is probably that of *Panopea glycymeris* which measures anything up to 30 cm in length. Like the Long-necked Clam it has a very long siphon, usually measuring more than twice the length of its shell. Again like the Long-necked Clam this siphon is encased in a leathery sheath. This species is not common enough to be fished commercially, but off the west coast of the United States the Pacific Geoduck *(Panopea generosa* Gould) is so highly esteemed as food that a limit is set on the number which may be gathered by one person in a day.

1 Long-necked Clam, *Mya arenaria* L.; 9·0 cm (shell only); northern hemisphere, widely distributed. **2** *Panopea glycymeris* L.; 20·0 cm; Mediterranean Prov. **3** *Ensis siliqua* L.; 12·0 cm; Boreal Prov

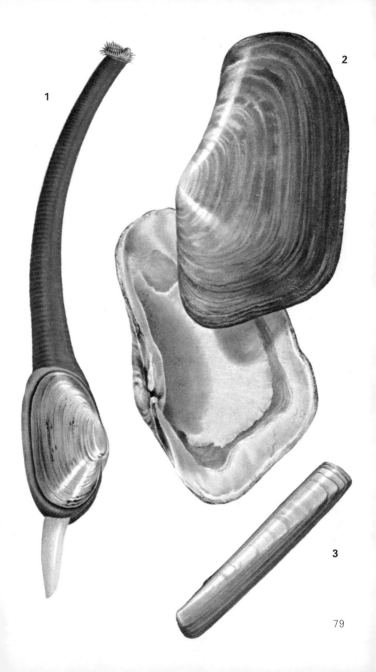

Shipworms and piddocks (Pholadacea)

Adapted for boring in wood, shipworms, such as *Teredo navalis*, are among the most destructive invertebrates in the world. They may perforate a wooden structure so completely that it collapses under stress. Each year they inflict enormous damage on wharf pilings, jetties and similar structures and when men sailed in wooden ships they lived in constant dread of sabotage by them. Their shells are much reduced and the two valves are not joined by a hinge. These are at one end of the long, shapeless body, the other end being provided with a pair of 'pallets' to close up that end of the burrow. The piddocks, many of which are adapted for boring in stone and clay, have larger shells but again the valves of these are not joined by a hinge.

Pandora's boxes (Pandoracea)

These bivalves and the

1 *Teredo navalis* L.; world-wide in fixed and floating timber. The tunnels are lined with shelly material. **2** *Brechites radix* Deshayes; 11·5 cm; (it is 3·0 cm wide at the top); Pacific. **3** *Halicardia flexuosa* Verrill & Smith; 4·1 cm; widely distributed in deep water

following two groups are nearly all fragile, colourless and, in one way or another, odd. Pandora's boxes have one of the valves deeply convex and the other almost flat.

Halicardia (Poromyacea)

The heart-shaped shell of *Halicardia flexuosa*, a widely distributed species from deep water, is strongly reminiscent of several unrelated bivalves, such as *Glossus humanus* (page 58) and *Corculum cardissa* (page 65).

Watering pots (Clavagellacea)

These must be the most un-bivalve-like bivalves in existence. A tiny embryonic pair of valves at the side of a mature specimen of *Brechites* shows that they start their lives conventionally. The mollusc then grows up into something strikingly different, something basically uni-valved. The end which sticks up out of the sea floor has an extraordinary resemblance to the 'rose' of a watering can. It is fitting that these most atypical of bivalves should be succeeded immediately by those molluscs which are characterized by the possession of a single shell apiece: the gastropods.

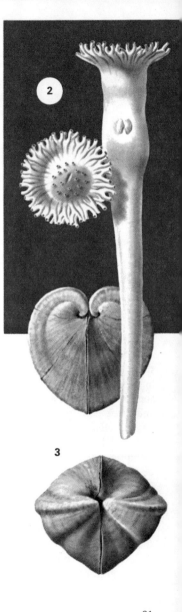

1 *Aplysia angasi* Sowerby; 28·0 cm; Indo-Pacific Prov. **2** *Scalenostoma lamberti* Souverbie; 2·1 cm; Pacific. **3** *Balcis martinii* A. Adams; 2·9 cm; Indo-Pacific Prov. **4** *Plotia terebellum* Müller; 3·5 cm; Pacific

Gastropods: Opisthobranchs
Bubble shells and their relatives

Perhaps no other major group of molluscs can show so much beauty and variety as this. Most of the species are shell-less and are known collectively – and rather unfairly – as sea slugs. Unquestionably these are among the loveliest objects in the sea. Their bodies are infinitely varied in shape with sometimes the most bizarre processes sprouting from them, and their colours are often breathtaking. Most of those that have shells, exquisite though these may be at times, cannot compare in beauty with those that are shell-less. With few exceptions the shells, when present, are extremely thin and brittle. Some species have internal shells and are usually swimmers, large lateral flaps being used as fins for this purpose. The only thick-shelled forms are nearly all small.

Bubble shells (the name is suggested by the bubble-like shape of most of them) are nearly all carnivores and swallow their prey alive. Often the prey is another mollusc and frequently one with a thick shell. This does not upset the carnivore whose gizzard is provided with a set of strong shelly plates or spines; shells are crushed between these plates and the animals which were previously enclosed within devoured. Although it is extremely unlikely that any member of this group is able to severely injure humans certain large shell-less kinds, known as sea hares *(Aplysia)*, have been known to cause temporary discomfort. Charles Darwin's journal of his voyage on the 'Beagle' tells of an encounter with a large one at St Jago, Cape Verde Islands, which had an acid secretion over its body; contact with this secretion caused a sharp stinging sensation like that produced by a jellyfish. It also emitted a purplish-red fluid which stained the water all around it, though this is a property common to many species in this group. *Aplysia angasi*, one of the largest species known, is the most striking of the several Australian members of the genus. *Balcis martinii* is a large representative of a widespread group of molluscs, which are mostly parasitic on other organisms and whose shells are usually tiny, slender, glossy and white. *Scalenostoma lamberti* is an oddly distorted relative of *Balcis*. It possesses a sharp keel which encircles each of the whorls.

Gastropods: Prosobranchs

In each member of this, the most extensive group of living molluscs, the auricle of the heart is in front of the ventricle, the visceral nerve loop is convoluted like a figure eight, and there are gills present. These features are internal and visible only after dissection. Externally the group's most obvious distinguishing feature is the presence of an operculum (though this is much reduced or absent in some). An operculum

1 Common Limpet, *Patella vulgata* L.; 5·3 cm; Boreal Prov. **2** Radula of Common Limpet, highly magnified. **3** *Zizyphinus zizyphinus* L.; 3·4 cm; Boreal-Mediterranean Provs. **4** Operculum of *Z. zizyphinus*. **5** Radula of *Z. zizyphinus*, highly magnified. **6 & 7** Outer and inner side (respectively) of operculum of *Turbo petholatus* L.; 2·0 cm. **8** Operculum of *Lambis lambis* L.; 2·5 cm. **9 & 10** Outer and inner side (respectively) of *Neritina communis* Quoy & Gaimard; 0·9 cm

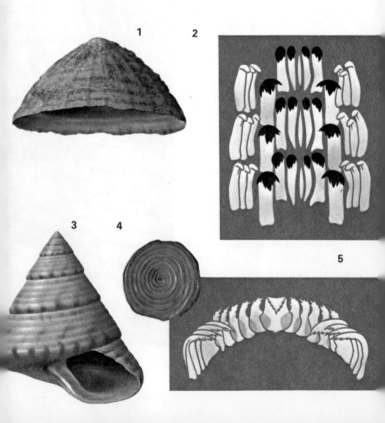

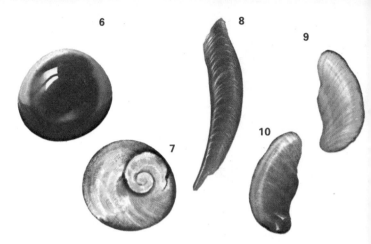

is also present in non-marine prosobranchs. There are several non-marine univalves which are smaller than the world's smallest prosobranchs, but the largest univalve in the world is a marine prosobranch with no near rival among the non-marine species.

The majority of the world's more attractive shells are prosobranchs and nearly all the collector's favourite groups are prosobranchs too. The more primitive ones, known as archaeogastropods (slit shells, limpets, top shells, nerites, etc.), have one or two gills and have a radula with many teeth in each row (indicating that they are herbivorous). The others, known as caenogastropods (periwinkles, ceriths, risso shells, wentletraps, cones, etc.), have a set of gills which are comb-like and the radula has few teeth to each row; these are omnivorous and include many voracious carnivores. The carnivorous propensities of many of them are frequently directed towards other molluscs, and bivalves are easy prey. In every way prosobranchs are more successful, more adaptable, and consequently more adventurous than bivalves (although there are some prosobranchs which are cemented in one position throughout their lives just like some of the bivalves). Altogether they have exploited far more ecological niches than have the bivalves and this is reflected in their more diverse shapes and sizes.

85

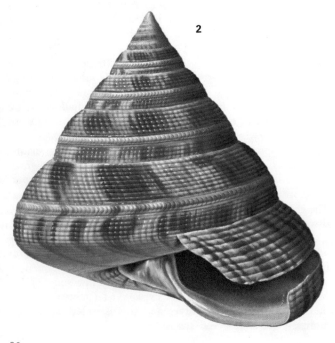

86

Slit shells (Pleurotomariacea)

These gastropods owe their popular name to the remarkable slit cut into the outer lip of their shells. Among the most primitive of all living gastropods, they discharge excrement into the water through the slit, thus preventing contamination of the gills. The dozen or so living species are nearly all colourful and some are very large. Fossil specimens have been known to science for a long time for these gastropods were extremely common many millions of years ago; living ones are now very scarce indeed. In 1855, when the first living specimen was brought up in a fisherman's pot in the Caribbean, scientists were amazed and delighted; here was a 'living fossil'. Others were dredged up some years later, but in the meantime two or three specimens of another species had turned up, also in the Caribbean. One of the finest specimens known was found, towards the end of the nineteenth century, on a shelf in a Barbados curio shop. Samuel Archer, the Englishman who found it, re-visited the shop several years later and there was another fine one on the same shelf! Known as Adanson's Slit Shell, *Entemnotrochus adansoniana* Crosse & Fischer, it is remarkable for its large size, the length of its slit, and for its wide and deep umbilicus. Rumpf's Slit Shell, *E. rumphii* Schepman, surpasses it in these respects. This giant species, averaging 18 cm in length and 15 cm in height, was first found in the 1870s in a miscellaneous collection of shells in Rotterdam. Despite its size it remained unique for a long time, one or two specimens being dredged up in the China Sea sixty years later. Since 1968 specimens trawled from deep water off Taiwan have come on to the market.

For many years the deep waters around Japan were the principal source of living slit shells, and *Mikadotrochus hirasei* is certainly the best known and now the easiest to acquire of all of them. In the early part of the twentieth century, however, the supply of specimens of this and related Japanese species (known as 'millionaire shells' by the fishermen) was never equal to the demand.

1 *Mikadotrochus beyrichi* Hilgendorf; 7·2 cm; Japan. **2** *M. hirasei* Pilsbry; 10·0 cm; Japan

Abalones (Pleurotomariacea)

These widely distributed molluscs are known by several alternative names: abalones (United States and Mexico), ear shells or sea ears (Australia and elsewhere in the Indo-Pacific), and ormers (Channel Islands off the north coast of France). Most of them live on rocky shores where they may be found scraping off the plant life covering the rocks. Their most noticeable feature is the single row of holes extending back from the edge of the aperture. As the creature grows it adds new, larger holes and seals up the earlier ones.

1 Ass's Ear, *Haliotis asinina* L.; 7·5 cm; Pacific. **2** *H. sanguinea* Hanley; 6·0 cm; S African Prov. **3** *Fissurella picta* Lamarck; 8·0 cm; Tierra del Fuego. **4** *Megathura crenulata* Sowerby; 12·0 cm; Californian Prov. **5** *Scutus unguis* L.; 5·0 cm; Pacific

A specimen is rarely found with a superfluity of holes, with no holes at all or with a slit in their place. Long feelers are thrust out through the holes, and de-oxygenated water is also expelled through them. Warm Australian waters harbour many different species including the Ass's Ear whose shell is used by natives for ornamental purposes. Very large species live in southern Californian waters and they are extensively fished there, about 1·5 million kg weight of the meat being gathered annually to satisfy the demand for abalone steaks. The shells of some species used to be the principal source of the small mother-of-pearl inlays which decorated the early

violin bows. Sometimes smothered with marine growth, an
abalone may be likened to a travelling zoo in which the
animals are mostly tiny and frequently molluscan.

Keyhole limpets (Pleurotomariacea)

In its use as an outlet for waste products the apical hole of
the keyhole limpets resembles the slit of the slit shells and
the holes of the abalones. The hole may resemble an old-
fashioned keyhole but usually it is elongate or circular.
Sometimes, as in the Great Keyhole Limpet, the hole is very

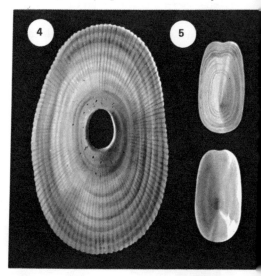

large, but in most species it is smaller relative to the overall
size of the shells.

Shield shells (Pleurotomariacea)

The shield shells are familiar objects on Australian shores
and are uninteresting when divorced from the animals.
Living specimens are most unusual, however, and are often
called elephant snails or elephant slugs. They are large and
black and have a snout vaguely similar to an elephant's
trunk; though ugly and slightly sinister in appearance they
are quite harmless.

True limpets (Patellacea)

Familiar objects on rocky shores in many parts of the world, the shells of true limpets can be distinguished from those of keyhole limpets by the absence of a hole at the apex. The flattened-cone shape of their shells enables them to resist the pounding of waves on exposed shores and, as anyone who has tried to remove one knows, the animal's foot acts like a powerful suction pad. Usually they feed at night, browsing on the algae-covered rocks and leaving characteristic radular teeth marks where they have fed. Some species are known to return to the same spot regularly after their feeding forays, and where the rock is fairly soft they gradually erode cavities into which they fit exactly. This is certainly true of limpets living on the west coast of France. Consequently students were puzzled by the discovery there,

1 *Patinigera magellanica* Gmelin (inside of shell); 5·5 cm; Magellanic Prov. **2** *Patella barbara* L.; 8·5 cm; S African Prov. **3** Common Limpet and its impression in soft rock; Boreal Prov. **4** *Cymbula compressa* L.; 6·0 cm; S African Prov

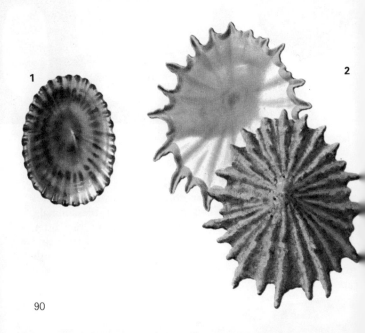

3

4

a few years ago, of a few specimens of the China Limpet (*Patella aspera* Lamarck) each of which carried young specimens of the same species. It was suggested that, for a time, the youngsters could find enough food on the mature limpets. With further growth they would have been unable to obtain sufficient food without moving further afield, and eventually each would have settled down on its own patch of rock. On the coasts of South Africa limpets grow fairly large and may be extremely abundant so that it is often difficult for young ones to settle except on the shells of mature specimens.

The subject of much experimental work and field observation, the Common Limpet is known to breed in winter on British coasts. Limpets living on the coasts of the United States, however, are all summer breeders as far as is known. Rough seas and strong winds may be factors in the Common Limpet's choice of a breeding season. Most limpets do not exceed 7 cm to 10 cm in length, but one attains giant proportions: *Patella mexicana* Broderip and Sowerby. This species, which inhabits the Panamic Province, may be 35 cm long and may weigh a few kilogrammes. The largest living limpet known, it is said to have been utilized as a wash-basin in Central America.

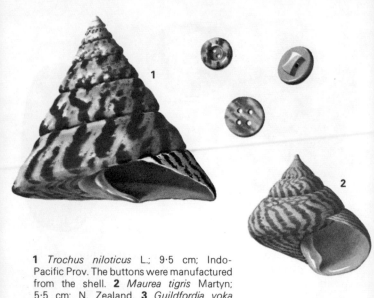

1 *Trochus niloticus* L.; 9·5 cm; Indo-Pacific Prov. The buttons were manufactured from the shell. 2 *Maurea tigris* Martyn; 5·5 cm; N. Zealand. 3 *Guildfordia yoka* Jousseaume; 10·0 cm; Japan. 4 *Angaria formosa* Reeve; 4·0 cm; Indo-Pacific Prov. 5 *Tristichotrochus formosensis* Smith; 6·0 cm; Taiwan

Top shells (Trochacea)

This extensive group is world-wide in distribution and includes pygmies 2 mm or 3 mm across as well as species several centimetres in height. They differ from the closely similar turban shells by having a thin, horny operculum instead of a thick, calcareous one. One of the larger species is *Trochus niloticus* which was once the essential raw material used in the manufacture of buttons. Ranging from the eastern Indian Ocean to Samoa, and from Queensland to Japan, it was hunted so relentlessly by divers during the period between the two world wars that it looked as though it could be exterminated by them. Fortunately its commercial value dropped almost to zero with the rise of the plastics industry and it is now hunted with far less zeal. The principal *Trochus* beds are found off the coasts of New Caledonia and Queensland and amongst the Andaman and Nicobar islands. The effects of over-fishing are obvious from the published figures showing the tonnage fished 'legally' (the overall tonnage, which includes that taken illegally by poachers, was almost certainly several times higher in each instance).

Queensland	New Caledonia	Andamans & Nicobar
1916: 1,048 tons	1913: 1,004 tons	1930: 450 tons
1922: 265 tons	1930: 180 tons	1935: 50 tons

As roughly 4,000 specimens comprise a ton it is probable that this mollusc, which takes more than three years to grow to a marketable size, would now be on the verge of extinction had not the world's greediest predator invented something far more lucrative to replace it.

Some top shells develop processes around the periphery, and in *Guildfordia yoka* these are extremely long and delicate. In *Angaria* the shell is considerably thickened, and the processes are also thick. *Tristichotrochus formosensis* used to be considered a rarity but it is now being obtained in large numbers from deep water off Taiwan. It is almost a pity that exquisite shells, such as this, should become commonplace.

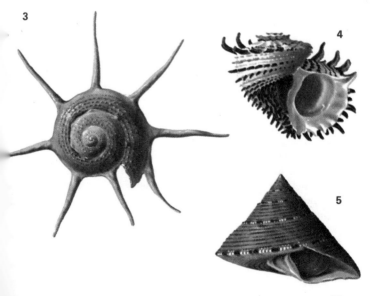

3

4

5

Turban shells (Trochacea)

In most respects the shells of this group resemble top shells, but turban shells have a thick, heavy operculum which is calcareous and not horny. The largest turban shell in the world, known as the Green Snail, has always been a favourite with collectors and has been fished commercially for many years. It is attractive enough in its natural state, but when its outer surface is removed (by acid or abrasion) a beautiful opalescent surface is exposed. Many articles, principally buttons and luxury items, used to be manufactured from it until, as with *Trochus niloticus*, plastics supplanted it. Its operculum is remarkably thick and heavy and makes an admirable paperweight. *Turbo petholatus* is another all-time favourite with collectors. The pretty opercula of this species, known as 'cat's eyes', are frequently picked up by beach-combers in the tropics, who are usually unaware that they were once part of a mollusc; earrings and many other objects have been made from them.

Pheasant shells and others (Trochacea)

Most of the pheasant shells are small and brightly coloured, the larger species being found in the Australian province. They have entirely porcellaneous shells, unlike those of top shells and turban shells which are always pearly within. They are also more elongated and are always smooth externally. The largest and most beautiful species is the Painted Lady, or Australian Pheasant, which is one of the most variable shells in the sea, as far as colour pattern is concerned. In this, and other related species, the animal progresses in a strange manner. When in motion the foot appears to be split longitudinally into two halves which advance alternately; one half remains stationary while the other moves forward, to be overtaken in turn by the previously stationary half. At one time shells of this species were considered very desirable, for like most molluscan shells restricted to the Australian province they were unknown in Europe until after one or

1 Two colour forms of the Painted Lady, *Phasianella australis* Gmelin; 6·2 cm; S Australia. **2** Green Snail, *Turbo marmoratus* L.; 15·0 cm; Indo-Pacific Prov. **3** *T. petholatus* L.; 6·5 cm; Indo-Pacific Prov

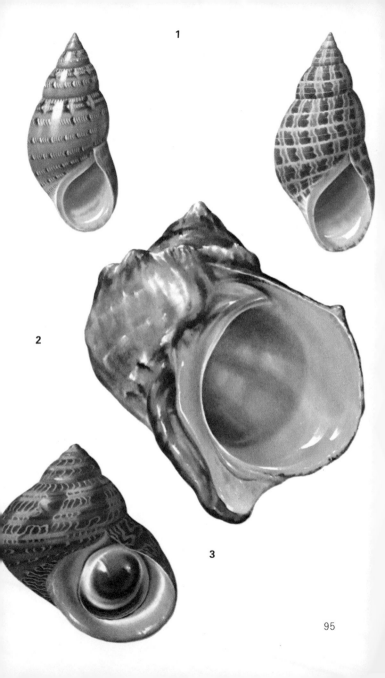

95

other of Captain Cook's voyages. The genus *Stomatia* occupies a systematic position somewhere between the top shells and turban shells, but none of its species has an operculum and their shells resemble miniature abalones.

Nerites (Neritacea)

The true nerites of the genus *Nerita* comprise mostly amphibious forms which frequent places liable to be uncovered at high tide. Abundantly represented in the tropics they include such familiar species as the Bleeding Tooth, that most aptly named of Caribbean shells. They have given rise to many species which have been able to colonize the brackish water near the mouths of rivers and, subsequently, the rivers themselves. *Neritodryas*, a genus well represented in Indo-

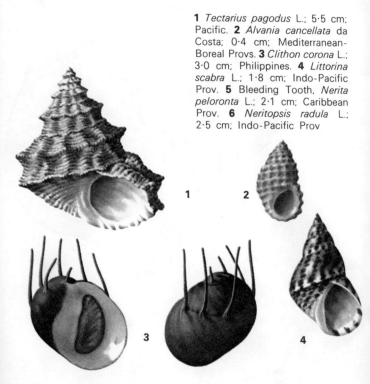

1 *Tectarius pagodus* L.; 5·5 cm; Pacific. **2** *Alvania cancellata* da Costa; 0·4 cm; Mediterranean-Boreal Provs. **3** *Clithon corona* L.; 3·0 cm; Philippines. **4** *Littorina scabra* L.; 1·8 cm; Indo-Pacific Prov. **5** Bleeding Tooth, *Nerita peloronta* L.; 2·1 cm; Caribbean Prov. **6** *Neritopsis radula* L.; 2·5 cm; Indo-Pacific Prov

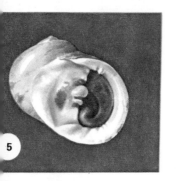

nesia, has become almost terrestrial in its habits. *Neritopsis* is chiefly remarkable for its solid operculum. Nerites are the ancestral forms of several tropical genera of prosobranch land snails.

Periwinkles (Littorinacea)
Periwinkles too are creatures which may be discovered in situations which may lead you to regard them as terrestrial. Typically inhabitants of rock pools, some periwinkles may live for long periods out of reach of the sea. They are not the swiftest of creatures, however, and so you would not expect to find them very far away from it. You would certainly not think of looking for them 120 m above it: but the common European Winkle *(Littorina littorea* L.) has been recorded at that altitude on a cliff at St Kilda in Scotland! Assuming that the specimens were identified correctly (and it has been suggested that they were not) one vital factor would have prevented them from becoming adapted to a thoroughly terrestrial way of life. They would have had to return to the sea to breed and deposit their eggs. As adults they can be as adventurous as they please, but their progeny must go through a free-swimming veliger stage. Thus parent and offspring are inescapably linked to the sea.

Risso shells (Rissoacea)
Risso shells, of which hundreds of species have been described, are all small or minute, and most are white in colour.

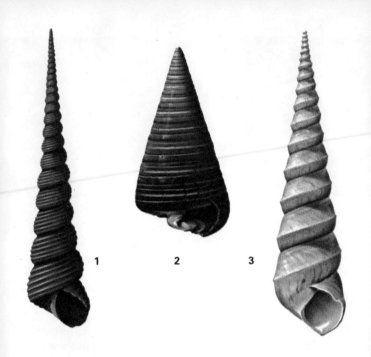

1   2   3

Screw shells and worm shells (Cerithiacea)

If conchologists had not examined the animals which constructed the shells shown here and on the following two pages, no-one could have proved that they are closely related to each other. Screw shells are beautiful examples of shells with many whorls which expand very gradually towards the aperture. In most respects, however, their contained animals resemble those of the flattened, rapidly expanding sundial shells illustrated on page 101. There is nothing particularly remarkable about the appearance of young worm shells; they look as if they are going to grow up with turreted or disc-like shells. After a while, however, they take an independent line and their further growth becomes a haphazard affair with the shell tube appearing to unwind and twist in different directions, rather like a worm. As a worm shell increases in size it vacates the hindmost portion of the shell and seals off the disused part by a transverse partition. The shells of some species closely resemble those of annelid worms (page 4).

Ceriths (Cerithiacea)

A tropical and subtropical group, ceriths have thick and usually nodulous shells and their apertures are widely expanded. With the exception of some small species all these shells are noteworthy for the unfinished appearance of their apertures. They always give the appearance of never having arrived at maturity. The many species show a bewildering variety of sculpture and colour although they are basically similar in shape. As there may also be great variation within a single species the group as a whole poses many problems of identification.

Tympanotonos radula and *Telescopium telescopium* are inhabitants of mud flats and mangrove swamps, the former a member of the West African province, the latter of the Indo-Pacific. *Telescopium telescopium* is particularly abundant in Indonesia and specimens may often be found in large swamps there grouped together with their apertures stuck into the mud and facing a common centre, the

4

1 *Turritella terebra* L.; 12·0 cm; Indo-Pacific Prov. **2** *Telescopium telescopium* L.; 9·0 cm; Indo-Pacific Prov. **3** *Turritella duplicata* L.; 15·0 cm; Indo-Pacific Prov. **4** *Tympanotonos radula* L.; 4·2 cm; W African Prov. **5** *Aletes squamigerus* Carpenter; 4·5 cm; Aleutian-Peruvian Provs

5

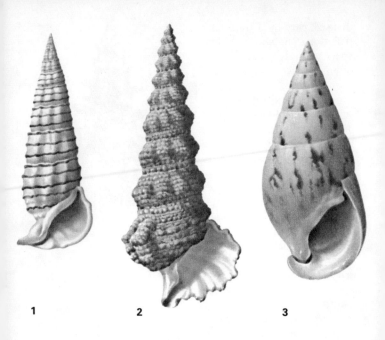

1 2 3

1 *Rhinoclavis asper* L.; 5·5 cm; Indo-Pacific Prov. 2 *Contumax nodulosus* Bruguière; 7·3 cm; Indo-Pacific Prov. 3 *Gourmya gourmyi* Crosse; 6·0 cm; Central Pacific. 4 *Cerithidea obtusa* Wood, suspended by mucus threads from a mangrove root; 4·0 cm; Indo-Pacific Prov. 5 Giant Creeper, *Campanile symbolicum* Iredale; 14·0 cm; SW Australia. 6 *Architectonica perspectiva* L.; 2·2 cm; Indo-Pacific Prov

apices pointing outwards like the spokes of a wheel. Natives of the Philippines and of some Indonesian islands long ago learnt how to make a meal out of this unsavoury-looking animal. After cooking it on wood fires they break off the top part of the spire and suck the animal's juices through the opening. *Cerithium nodulosum*, a coral-reef dweller, is one of the larger and better known species, and *Gourmya gourmyi* one of the lesser known; the former is notably rough and knobbly, the latter comparatively smooth. In size the Giant Creeper greatly outstrips all other living ceriths. Whitish and heavy, it looks like a fossil, and this appearance of antiquity fooled no less a man than the French naturalist-philosopher, Lamarck. In 1810 he bought the first specimen ever seen in Europe, from a colleague. A few years earlier he had described as new to science an enormous fossil cerith, *Campanile giganteum,* and he concluded that his new shell was the same as this fossil. As the fossil was supposed to have been extinct for millions of years the discovery of a living example was of great interest. Although apparently closely related to the fossil, the Giant Creeper is now considered to be a different species. The much smaller *Cerithidea obtusa* is remarkable for the way in which it suspends itself upside-down by means of mucous threads secreted by its foot.

4

Sundials (Cerithiacea)

The shells of sundials have little resemblance to ceriths and screw shells but they are closely related anatomically. Abundant as fossils, there are relatively few living species and nearly all of them

5

6

1

are found in the Indo-Pacific Province. The structure of the inside edge of the whorls as seen in the umbilicus has earned them the alternative popular name 'winding staircases'.

Wentletraps (Epitoniacea)

Of the many living wentletrap species the majority have almost colourless shells but nearly all are exquisitely sculptured with prominent, regularly-spaced ribs. It is this sculptural feature, the hallmark of the group, which endears wentletraps to collectors and has given inspiration to artists and designers. Large specimens of the Precious Wentletrap still bring high prices at auction.

Hairy shells and cap shells (Calyptraeacea)

The periostracum of the cold-water hairy shells is so highly developed in some species

2

1 Precious Wentletrap, *Epitonium scalare* L.; 5·8 cm; Indo-Pacific Prov. **2** Hungarian Cap, *Capulus ungaricus* L.; 5·4 cm; Boreal Prov. **3** *Calyptraea chinensis* L.; 1·7 cm; Boreal Prov. **4** *Trichotropis bicarinata* Sowerby; 4·0 cm; Arctic seas. **5** *Amathina tricarinata* L.; 2·3 cm; Indian Ocean. **6** *Vanikoro cancellata* Lamarck; 2·0 cm; Indo-Pacific Prov

that it forms a tough, hairy coating over the shells. In *Trichotropis bicarinata*, the largest of the hairy shells, the keels around the periphery are ornamented with long periostracal processes which peel off in very dry storage conditions. A thick periostracum is a characteristic feature of some cap shells and is well seen in the Hungarian Cap. This species, which has an extensible proboscis, often attaches itself to the edge of a bivalve mollusc and helps itself to the food supply of its host.

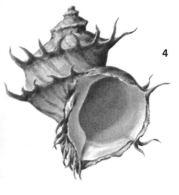

Cup-and-saucer limpets (Calyptraeacea)

The 'shelf' on the inside surface of *Calyptraea chinensis* is characteristic of the cup-and-saucer limpets; in some species the shelf is literally cup-shaped.

Vanikoro and Amathina (Amalthacea)

The totally dissimilar shells of *Vanikoro* and *Amathina* house animals which are closely related anatomically. There are many instances among molluscs of dissimilar shells housing closely related animals; but unrelated molluscs with similar shells are met with much more often.

Carrier shells (Strombacea)

Several different kinds of gastropods and a few bivalves attach the shells of other molluscs, as well as heavy foreign bodies such as stones, to their own shells. Only in the genus *Xenophora* is this shell-collecting faculty highly developed. Shells of this genus are usually smothered with other shells which we may presume have the effect, if not the purpose, of camouflage. When stones are utilized they may weigh two or three times as much as the shell and animal combined. *X. pallidula* utilizes almost any kind of shell but seems to affix each kind in a certain way. Long, pointed gastropod shells stick out like the spokes of a wheel, and the valves of bivalves are arranged around the edge with their outer sides facing downwards. Obviously a shell so encumbered would present problems to the contained animal if it tried to crawl along a sandy sea bed. Fortunately a carrier shell's method of locomotion prevents it from digging itself into the sand; it moves along in a series of leaps. Its muscular foot is thrust out and the strong, semicircular operculum is jabbed into the sand; by pulling against this anchorage the whole animal is jerked forwards in such a way that it leaps over the sea bed and so avoids embedding itself. The strombs and scorpion shells move in a similar fashion. *Stellaria solaris*, which attaches sand grains to its embryonic shell, used to be a great prize for collectors, particularly if its spines were intact.

Struthiolaria and Terebellum (Strombacea)

Struthiolaria shells, which are almost confined to New Zealand waters, burrow into sand when feeding. *Terebellum terebellum* also burrows in sand but it is not known if it does so for feeding purposes. When burrowing it has one or other of its stalked eyes above the sand surface, each eye taking it in turns to survey the watery world above. Although it may remain stationary for a long time it has been seen to leap

1 *Terebellum terebellum* L.; 4·3 cm (shell only); Indo-Pacific Prov. **2** *Stellaria solaris* L.; 8·5 cm; Indo-Pacific Prov. **3** *Tugurium exutum* Reeve; 7·0 cm; Indo-Pacific Prov. **4** *Struthiolaria papulosa* Martyn; 7·8 cm; N. Zealand. **5** *Xenophora pallidula* Reeve; 4·5 cm; Indo-Pacific Prov

several centimetres from the ground and will do so quite unexpectedly if held in the palm of the hand.

Strombs (Strombacea)

Wherever the sea is warm enough to allow coral reefs to flourish you will probably find strombs flourishing too. Of the fifty or more living species about forty are found in the Indo-Pacific. A mature stromb is immediately recognizable as such because it has a 'stromboid notch' on the edge of the outer lip near the lower (i.e. anterior) end. Through this notch the stalked right eye protrudes, the stalk of that eye being usually shorter than the left eye stalk. The world's largest

Queen Conch, *Strombus gigas* L.; 23·0 cm; Caribbean Prov

1 Pelican's Foot *Aporrhais pes-pelecani* L.; 4·5 cm; Boreal Prov.
2 Juvenile stage of Pelican's Foot

1   **2**

species, and one of the rarer, is *Strombus goliath* Schroeter. This largest of Brazilian shells reaches a length of 32·5 cm. Rather smaller, but still the world's second largest stromb, is the Queen Conch of the Caribbean. It is a favourite with collectors and curio dealers, and florists sell it for flower-arranging purposes. Because it is abundant and the animal is highly esteemed as food it is gathered in vast numbers annually. On the beaches of some Caribbean islands there are huge mounds of them. Unfortunately every shell has a hole in the spire which was made to facilitate removal of the animal. The shells are sometimes crushed to form a powder used in the manufacture of porcelain, and good quality specimens can also be utilized for the manufacture of cameos. Fine pink pearls are found in them occasionally. These were once considered extremely valuable but are regarded less highly nowadays. The young shells of some strombs may resemble cone shells and have fooled experts. Young shells of the Pelican's Foot are also very different from mature ones.

Scorpion shells (Strombacea)

These large and often heavy shells are found in the warmest parts of the Indo-Pacific. Nearly all of the nine species are distinguished from other shells by the long 'spines' on the outer lip, but young scorpion shells lack these outgrowths

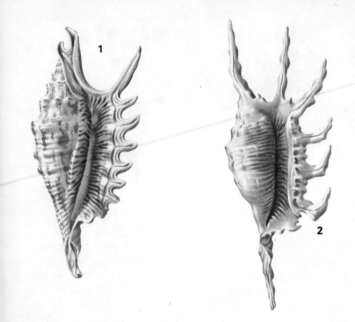

and resemble very different gastropods. As in the strombs the operculum is sickle-shaped and is used to help the animal lever itself off the ground when moving forwards. *Lambis truncata* is the largest species, specialists distinguishing two forms (or sub-species) one of which has a flat apex, the other a pointed apex. The two forms inhabit different areas and do not intermingle; but both are eaten raw or roasted by natives. Male scorpion shells differ from females in size, sculpture and the nature of the spines. In some species the male may be as much as forty-five per cent smaller than the female. *Lambis scorpius* is one of the longer-spined species while *Lambis digitata* has the spines so reduced that they are stumpy by comparison.

1 *Lambis digitata* Perry; 12·5 cm; Indo-Pacific Prov. **2** *L. scorpius* L.; 15·0 cm; SW Pacific. **3** *L. truncata sebae* Kiener; 30·0 cm; Indo-Pacific Prov. **4** Immature shell of *L. truncata truncata* Lightfoot; 15·0 cm; Indo-Pacific Prov. This sub-species occupies a different geographical region from the previous one.

Lamellarias (Lamellariacea)

In life the lamellarias are flattened and slug-like, their low-spired shells being enveloped by the animal. The Transparent Lamellaria has an extremely thin and fragile shell which cannot conceivably give it any protection.

Trivias and others (Triviacea)

Trivias, which should not be confused with the true cowries, resemble lamellarias in their feeding habits, for both feed on tunicates. Unlike true cowries the trivias have prominent

1 Poached Egg Cowry, *Ovula ovum* L.; 8·0 cm; Indo-Pacific Prov.
2 Transparent Lamellaria, *Lamellaria perspicua* L.; 1·2 cm; Boreal Prov.
3 Little Egg Cowry, *Calpurnus verrucosus* L.; 2·8 cm; Indo-Pacific
4 Elongated Egg Cowry, *Volva volva* L.; 10·5 cm; Indo-Pacific Prov.
5 *Trivia californiana* Gray; 1·0 cm; Californian Prov. **6** *Erato lachryma* Sowerby; 0·7 cm; Pacific

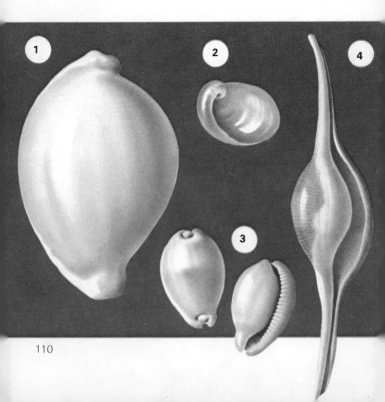

ridges on the surface of the shell. Even though the mantle folds extend up over it the shell is not glossy like most of the cowries. Erato shells, some of which do not exceed 3 mm in length, also cover their shells with their mantle folds. Pedicularias attach themselves very securely to coral stalks, and they are difficult to detect because they are often the same colour as the coral, usually a deep red.

Egg cowries (Cypraeacea)

With its pure white exterior and deep chocolate-brown interior the Poached Egg Cowry is one of the outstanding shells of the Indo-Pacific. The animal, a deep velvety black in colour with white papillae scattered over it, sets off the whiteness of the shell in a startling fashion. Shells of this species have been employed by man in many ways throughout its range and even beyond. Apparently it is even preferred to the true cowries as a fertility symbol. The prows of fishing vessels are often adorned with rows of the shells, and they are used extensively for personal adornment. The Elongated Egg Cowry resembles the Poached Egg Cowry but has more attenuated ends. The Little Egg Cowry contains a white animal with black spots – the exact opposite of the animal of the Poached Egg Cowry – and again the shell is widely utilized by natives for decorative purposes.

5

6

Cowries (Cypraeacea)

Of all the natural objects living in the world's oceans these are probably the most desirable and certainly among the most costly. Glossy, colourful and smooth they have been attractive to men and women since prehistoric times, and their popularity increases daily. Many collectors are interested in them to the exclusion of all other shells and will often pay high prices for specimens new to their collections. Largely tropical in their distribution, cowries are especially common in the vicinity of coral reefs, and in some places their abundance is astonishing. It is not surprising that they have been utilized in many different ways by man. One of them, the Money Cowry, has been a familiar form of currency over a large part of the world since time immemorial and shells of this and related tropical species have been unearthed from archaeological sites in Central Europe and the Caucasus. It has also been widely used for decorative purposes, particularly by certain tribes in Africa. Its monetary value differed from place to place, great quantities being required to complete some transactions. In the early nineteenth century a European living at Cuttack on the north-east coast of India decided to pay for the erection of his bungalow entirely in cowries; sixteen million were required!

Young shells of most cowry species are thinner than mature ones and their colouring differs too. This is because they lack the successive layers of enamel which would be deposited by the animal's mantle (which in cowries covers the whole shell). By buffing down mature shells the underlying layers are revealed. Long ago shell dealers successfully peddled buffed down and re-polished common cowries as different species. This practice is not extinct even now. Unsuspecting tourists visiting Fiji are currently being offered buffed down specimens of the Humpback Cowry (under the name 'Tapa Cowry') and other species. The price asked for the fakes is

1 *Cypraea argus* L.; 8·0 cm; Indo-Pacific Prov. 2 *C. stolida* L.; 2·6 cm; Indo-Pacific Prov. 3 *C. ziczac* L.; 2·0 cm; Indo-Pacific Prov. 4 Money Cowry, *C. moneta* L.; 2·6 cm; Indo-Pacific Prov. 5 African mask, decorated with shells of Money Cowry. 6 *C. carneola* L.; 5·0 cm; Indo-Pacific Prov. 7 Humpback Cowry, *C. mauritiana* L.; 9·2 cm; Indo-Pacific Prov

1
2
3
4
5
6
7

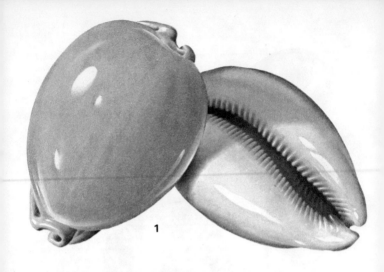

1 Golden Cowry, *Cypraea aurantium* Gmelin; 9·0 cm; SW Pacific.
2 Fulton's Cowry, *C. fultoni* Sowerby; 5·0 cm; S African Prov. **3**
Spotted Cowry, *C. guttata* Gmelin; 6·0 cm; SW Pacific. **4** Hirase's
Cowry, *C. hirasei* Roberts; 5·0 cm; Japan

several times higher than that asked for the genuine articles!
Admittedly many cowries are very attractive to human eyes
but it is something of a mystery why they have so universal
an appeal. It is well known that they were once widely appre-
ciated as symbols of fertility and it is reasonable to suggest
that their continuing appeal may have a sexual foundation.

Rare cowries
Next to the Glory-of-the-Sea Cone the most familiar shell
rarity is the Golden Cowry (also known as the Morning Dawn
or Orange Cowry). Unlike the cone this shell is one of the
outstanding beauties of its genus; once seen it cannot be confused with any other shell. It is not really rare as there are
hundreds in collections at the present time, but every collector
wants it and so the supply is never equal to the demand. The
darling of every shell auction, it sometimes comes up for sale
with a hole in one side. This indicates that it once adorned the
person of a Pacific islander (if a label accompanies such a shell

the locality almost always reads 'Fiji'). Inhabitants of several island groups in the south-west Pacific used to wear it as a mark of distinction. In the Loyalty Islands it used to be looked upon with superstitious awe; at the end of the nineteenth century it was solemnly asserted by the natives that a woman who found one died after having been struck on the forehead by a 'demon' who did not approve of her taking it.

Although few cowries are as strikingly attractive as the Golden Cowry several are more highly prized by collectors. Among the more desirable of these is the Spotted Cowry of which only about sixteen specimens were recorded prior to 1963, and although others have been found since then they always bring high prices. Fulton's Cowry is difficult to obtain because it is usually found in the stomachs of certain deep-water fish. Hirase's Cowry has been a top priority with collectors for many years. The White-toothed Cowry *(Cypraea leucodon* Broderip), of which five specimens are known at present, must rank as one of the world's most valuable objects.

2

3

4

Heteropods

These strange molluscs are the only prosobranchs which can be considered true swimmers *(Ianthina* is powerless to move itself in a particular direction and merely drifts passively). Their shells are extremely thin, fragile and transparent; and some species have no shell at all. Largest of all heteropods, *Carinaria cristata* has a conical shell with a tiny apical knob; the animal, which is ridiculously large by comparison, normally swims upside down with the shell underneath. For many years the shell of this mollusc was highly prized by collectors who thought that it must be a small *Nautilus.* Even well into the nineteenth century it was considered the rarest of all shells and brought correspondingly high prizes at auction. It is now considered a curiosity without commercial value.

Necklace shells (Naticacea)

The shells of this group of molluscs are as thick and strong as those of heteropods are thin and weak. Most necklace shells prey upon bivalves, which explains why so many otherwise perfect bivalve shells have a neat bevelled hole in them when they are found on the beach. An acid secretion from a small gland near the tip of the proboscis softens up the shell and the animal then works away at the softened material with its radula. These molluscs adopt an unusual method of depositing their eggs. A necklace-like string of eggs is produced and sand grains are then incorporated into this string so that it becomes firm but pliable. These coiled egg ribbons may often be seen lying on sandy beaches. A striking feature of many necklace shells is the way in which shelly matter is deposited in the region of the umbilicus. In some species, such as *Neverita josephinia,* a brown 'plug' is formed, while in others, such as *Polynices mamilla,* the umbilicus is completely obliterated by growth of the shell. The operculum in this group is often sculptured in a most attractive manner. Some species have striking colour patterns on their shells, but in general the group is noteworthy for the similarity of many of its species. Unfortunately, this means that it is often extremely difficult to decide to which species a particular specimen belongs.

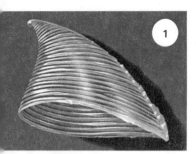

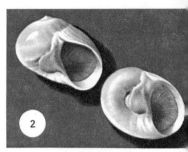

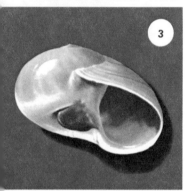

1 *Carinaria cristata* L.; 9·0 cm; Pacific. **2** *Neverita josephinia* Risso;
3·0 cm; Mediterranean Prov. **3** *Polynices duplicatus* Say; 4·2 cm;
Transatlantic-Caribbean Provs.

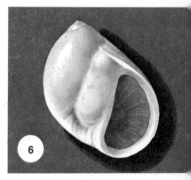

4 *Globularia fluctuata* Sowerby; 5·4 cm; Philippines. **5** Egg ribbon of
P. duplicatus. **6** *P. mamilla* L.; 5·5 cm; Indo-Pacific Prov.

Helmet shells and others (Tonnacea)

The molluscs discussed on pages 118 to 123 are related to each other anatomically and many of them have similar habits, but their shells show an astonishing diversity of form, sculpture and colour pattern. For many years conchologists were accustomed to arranging specimens in the cabinet according to a system based on shell characters. This meant that many shells of unrelated animals were grouped together. Many living molluscs, particularly the smaller ones, are still known to us only by their shells, and it is certain that some of them are incorrectly positioned in even the most highly organized museum collections.

No closely related molluscs could have shells more different from each other than *Distorsio* and *Morum,* the former being deformed and ugly, the latter exquisitely sculptured and attractive. Several *Morum* species are rare as well as attractive and are considered desirable. *M. praeclarum*, for instance, is known from a single shell, and nobody knows where that one was found. Helmet shells, which provide the cameo cutter with his favourite raw material, flourish best in warm seas, the larger ones being found only in tropical waters. *Cassidaria echinophora* is one of those found in temperate waters as is suggested by its lack of bright colouring. *Phalium glaucum* exhibits a feature common to many helmet shells and their relatives: a series of flange-like ribs (or 'varices', singular 'varix'). Some species have very pronounced varices (which are merely the protruding edges of former apertural lips) the spacing of which differs from one species to another but seems to be fairly constant in specimens of a single species. If a number of different helmet shells is inspected closely, preferably from above the apex of each shell, several types of varical arrangements may be distinguished. These different arrangements presumably indicate that the animals concerned have different modes of life and that their growth rates differ.

1 *Distorsio clathrata* Lamarck; 8·5 cm; N Carolina - Caribbean Prov. **2** *Phalium glaucum* L.; 9·0 cm; Indo-Pacific Prov. **3** *Morum cancellatum* Sowerby; 4·9 cm; SE Asia. **4** *Cassidaria echinophora* L.; 6·0 cm; Mediterranean Prov. **5** *Morum praeclarum* Melvill; 3·7 cm; locality unknown

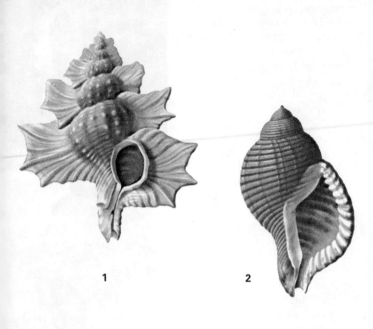

1 Winged Frog, *Biplex perca* Perry; 5·7 cm; W Pacific. **2** *Linatella cingulata* Lamarck; 4·7 cm; Indo-Pacific Prov. **3** *Ficus ficoides* Lamarck; 9·0 cm (shell only); Indo-Pacific Prov

Frog shells (Tonnacea)

Most of the predominantly tropical frog shells have heavy, rough shells with prominent, regularly-spaced varices. As they live in rocky situations the varices, which have a strengthening effect, have probably been developed to help the creatures withstand the many hard knocks that they must receive. They have a hard and horny operculum which, presumably, gives them additional protection in rough weather. *Linatella cingulata* is a rotund, relatively smooth-shelled species, and *Biplex perca,* sometimes known as the Winged Frog, looks as though it has been squashed flat. There are some frog shells which are much larger than the two just mentioned and a few attain an overall length of nearly 30 cm.

Fig shells (Tonnacea)

The shells of these sand-dwelling molluscs bear no resemblance to those of the frog shells. They are thin and fragile and devoid of varices, and they also lack any kind of operculum. Although they have a certain elegance they are not colourful and there is little variation from species to species. The uninspiring appearance of the shells, however, belies the beauty of the living mollusc, as is shown in our pictures of *Ficus ficoides*. Bearing its light shell gracefully and easily,

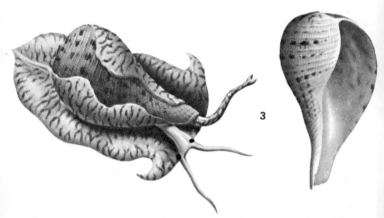

3

the creature crawls rapidly along, its siphons erect, its foot expanded like a broad and flattened disc, its large, bright, black eyes peering out from its long, flat head, and its slim tentacles stretched out to the fullest extent. It also has a long proboscis but this is rarely exserted when crawling along. It can be seen also that the mantle covers the sides of the shell, as it does in the cowries and margin shells. Comparing the picture of the shell of *Ficus ficoides* with that of the complete mollusc it is at once evident that the study of shells is greatly enhanced if you also study the animals which make them. It is sometimes easy to forget that a shell was once part of a living, moving creature: it is impossible to forget the spectacle of a living mollusc, such as *Ficus ficoides*, when it is discovered on the march in its native habitat. A shell collector who becomes a student of living molluscs has much to gain.

He may not enlarge his cabinet but he will enlarge his mind.

Tun shells (Tonnacea)

Some of the world's most capacious shells belong in this group. The larger tun shells are seldom seen in collections because their size and fragility make them troublesome to handle and difficult to store. Also they are hard to come by in the first place as they are inhabitants of fairly deep water. *Tonna melanostoma* is the most attractive of these giant molluscs, its shell being distinguished from all others by a dark chocolate-brown columella. Off-shore waters of New South Wales have produced two or three outsized species, the largest of them being nick-named the Beer Barrel *(Tonna cerevisina* Hedley); exceptionally its shell can hold over two litres of liquid (occasionally the shell of a Mediterranean species, *Tonna galea* L., is even more capacious). In the middle of the nineteenth century John MacGillivray, a Scottish naturalist, found some minute molluscs floating in mid-ocean; each of them had long tentacle-like processes protruding from the aperture, unlike any other mollusc of comparable size known at that time. Later they were named *Macgillivrayia pelagica* by Edward Forbes, a distinguished fellow naturalist who had a specialized knowledge of molluscs. Shortly afterwards, however, the French conchologist Paul Fischer suggested that they were merely the free-swimming larvae of an unknown species of tun shell. Fischer was right; it is now well known that the larvae of tun shells and their relatives have processes such as Forbes described. It is also known that these molluscs have a long free-swimming stage and can drift great distances. But all this was unknown to Forbes and most of his contemporaries, and other larval forms were erroneously described as new species by equally competent naturalists.

Trumpet shells (Tonnacea)

Many different kinds of gastropod shells have been utilized as trumpets but the shell of the Pacific Triton is the best

1 *Tonna melanostoma* Jay; 17·0 cm; Central Pacific. **2** Pacific Triton, *Charonia tritonis* L.; 36·0 cm; Indo-Pacific Prov

123

known of them. One of the world's larger gastropods, it is very widely distributed throughout the Indo-Pacific. In the Society Islands many years ago large shells of this species were selected for use as trumpets. A hole 2·5 cm wide was made near the shell's apex and a bamboo cane, about 90 cm long, was inserted, secured with braid and gummed into place. Such trumpets were blown on important occasions, such as the inauguration of kings and the commencement of battle.

Murex shells (Muricacea)

These are carnivorous creatures which live in tropical and temperate waters. Elaborate spiny outgrowths seen in many species immediately distinguish them from all other gastropods. As the spines are hollow and can become filled with mud and sand they should be avoided by anyone with bare feet. Among the spiniest of all shells is

1 *Pterynotus alatus* Röding; 7·0 cm; W Pacific. **2** Thorny Woodcock, *Murex pecten* Lightfoot; 12·0 cm; W Pacific. **3** *Poirieria zealandia* Quoy & Gaimard; 6·0 cm; N. Zealand. **4** *Chicoreus steeriae* Reeve; 7·5 cm; Central Pacific. **5** Staghorn Murex, *Euphyllon cornucervi* Röding; 8·5 cm; W Pacific

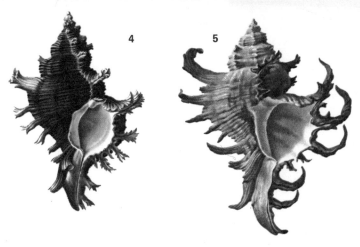

4   5

the Thorny Woodcock or Venus's Comb, a species which has been a favourite with collectors for centuries. Undoubtedly such a shell is well protected from large predators although, surprisingly, some fishes seem to be unharmed after swallowing and digesting similar shells. The small, tooth-like structure seen on the outer lip of the Thorny Woodcock is insignificant compared with that of some of its relatives. In several species this tooth is larger and much more conspicuous. One Pacific species has been seen to drag an ark shell out of its hiding place and insert the tooth between the valves to prevent them closing; the ark shell was then eaten. Many species prey on bivalves by forcing the valves apart with the foot acting as a suction pad and the apertural lip acting as a lever. Instead of boring neat holes in the shells of their victims some murex shells chip the edges of the valves to make a small opening and suck the animal's juices through it. In the Gulf of California as many as five large murex shells (*Muricanthus nigritus* Philippi) have been seen attacking a single live clam all at the same time.

The Staghorn Murex owes its popular name to the way in which its spines curl back to resemble antlers. The purple-tipped fronds of *Murex steeriae* are quite different in character. Like so many tropical shells the beautiful colouring of freshly collected specimens fades if exposed to the light for long periods. *Pterynotus alatus* is devoid of spines and colour but

captivates all who see it. Instead of spines it has a series of longitudinal varices which seem to twist around the shell.

Murex shells and the Royal Purple

Mediterranean murex shells are humdrum compared with the tropical ones illustrated on the previous two pages, but two of them have made a far greater impact on the affairs of man: *Bolinus brandaris* and *Hexaplex trunculus*. These two molluscs are the principal source of the dye which came to be known as the Royal Purple. At least 2,000 years before the Christian era it was known that a colour-fast dye could be procured from a special gland common to these two species (their eggs were also a rich source of the dye). The economy of the Phoenicians living along the eastern seaboard of the Mediterranean depended on the manufacture and sale of cloth impregnated with it. Large mounds containing incalculable numbers of broken shells may be seen today between Mount Carmel and Sidon along the coast of Lebanon. Wicker baskets baited with offal were set in the sea to attract and ensnare the molluscs and the catch was dealt with at once, larger shells being cracked open and the all-important gland extracted by hand; the rest were probably subjected to a mass crushing operation.

Contrary to popular belief the dye so obtained varied greatly in hue, according to the processing method adopted, but was usually somewhere in the range from deep reddish-black to violet. That resembling the amethyst gemstone was highly prized by the Romans. The purple industry was still lingering on during Charlemagne's reign in the eighth century but died out soon after. This is not surprising. Recently it was demonstrated that 12,000 *B. brandaris* yield approximately 1·5 grams of crude dye, or about sufficient to colour the fringe of a lady's dress. An astronomical number of specimens would be required to deal with the entire garment. It is no accident

1 *Hexaplex trunculus* L.; 6·8 cm; Mediterranean Prov. **2** Specimen of *H. trunculus* from shell mound at Sidon showing where shell was broken to remove the tissues. **3** *Bolinus brandaris* L.; 8·5 cm; Mediterranean Prov. Purple coloration indicates sites where the purple-dye industry flourished.

1 *Rapana venosa* Valenciennes; 11·0 cm; Japan, and introduced into the Black Sea. **2** *Nassa serta* Bruguière; 3·2 cm; Indo-Pacific Prov. **3** *Forreria belcheri* Hinds; 10·0 cm; Californian Prov. **4** *Columbarium pagoda* Lesson; 8·0 cm; Japan. **5** *Drupa elegans* Broderip; 2·4 cm; Central Pacific. **6** Mawe's Latiaxis, *Latiaxis mawae* Griffith & Pidgeon; 4·2 cm; Japan. **7** *Trophon geversianum* Pallas; 8·0 cm; Magellanic Prov

that imperial robes and many other garments associated with pomp and majesty are purple in colour.

Drupes, latiaxis and pagoda shells (Muricacea)

The external appearance of most of the Indo-Pacific drupes is disappointing because these shells are nearly always worn and encrusted with coral growths. The apertures of most of them, however, are colourful, polished and ornamented. Latiaxis shells are most commonly found in deep water around Japan. Like so many Japanese shells they are reminiscent of certain architectural features associated with that country. Mawe's Latiaxis was one of the first to be discovered and is still a collector's item. The Common Pagoda is also found around Japan and again seems somehow Japanese in its structure.

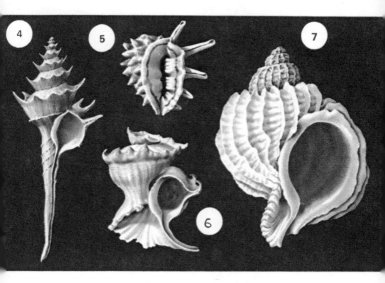

Trophons and rapana shells (Muricacea)

The trophons are mostly cold-water molluscs and include several species which have an insatiable appetite for commercially exploitable bivalves. *Trophon geversianum*, the largest and handsomest species, is noteworthy for the frill-like lamellae (which are rarely as perfect as in the Falkland Islands specimen illustrated here). The animal has been known to drill a hole through the shell of a mussel in two and a half hours. A native of Japanese waters *Rapana venosa* is now being anxiously studied well away from its original home. In 1947 it was noticed in the Black Sea where it has become abundant. It now threatens to eliminate the entire shell-fish industry there and has already destroyed enormous banks of oysters. When oysters are not available Black Sea specimens of this voracious predator (which are smaller than most Japanese ones) can keep alive by devouring smaller molluscs. It is also known that *R. venosa* can withstand very unfavourable conditions, such as lowered salinity and variable temperatures, and is extremely fertile, as many as 377,000 eggs being laid by a single female in one summer. Evidently this unwelcome visitor has discovered a perfect refuge for

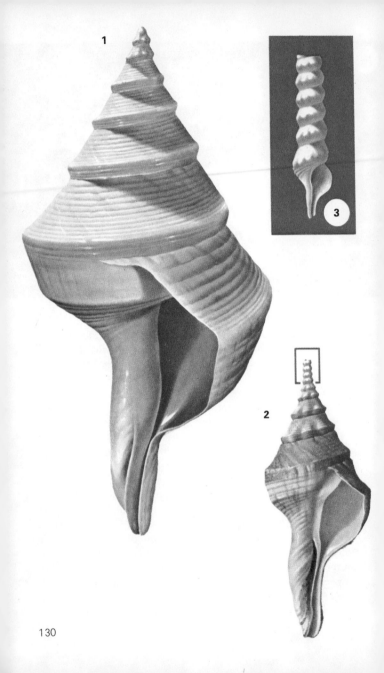

130

itself in its new environment. Should it spread to the Mediterranean and the Atlantic Ocean the consequences to the shell-fish industries of those seas could be disastrous.

Whelks (Buccinacea)

The most extensive, most varied group of gastropods is that which may be loosely designated the whelk group. It includes hundreds of different species and some of these are so abundant in places that they may be collected by the millions (and of certain edible species millions are collected annually). Nearly all whelks are carnivorous and live on dead fish and similar offal. The majority of species are undoubtedly drab, but there are some attractive and unusual features to be found in many others, especially in their shape and sculpture. Some are distinguished above all by their size, for this group includes the world's largest gastropods. The False Trumpet Shell is the largest and probably the most voluminous gastropod shell in the world. When fresh it is covered with a thick periostracum, and this peels off when dry to reveal a smooth, polished shell of a pale apricot colour. An inhabitant of the Indo-Pacific it is utilized by natives of northern Australia and elsewhere for domestic and ceremonial purposes.

The eggs are deposited in a tough, rectangular mass of fan-shaped capsules about 20 cm long and 10 cm wide. The youngsters emerging from these capsules are totally unlike their parents, and the dissimilarity fooled G. W. Tryon and H. A. Pilsbry, two of the world's foremost conchologists in their day. In 1887 Tryon described them as a new species of *Cerithium*; and seven years later Pilsbry not only based the description of another new species on them but created a new genus for both! For a short time the curious embryonic shell stays attached to the maturing one and then falls off. Tryon and Pilsbry should not be criticized for their blunders; neither had seen a young shell with its curious embryo still attached, and no-one could be expected to guess that the embryo and the adult were once intimately connected.

1 False Trumpet Shell, *Syrinx aruana* L.; 50·0 cm; Pacific. **2** An immature specimen with embryonic shell attached; 13·5 cm. **3** Embryonic shell

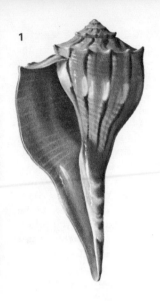

Fulgur whelks
(Buccinacea)

The fulgur whelks are interesting not just because they are large, which most of them are, but because some are right-handed and some are left-handed in their coiling. The existence of right-handed and left-handed species in the same genus is a phenomenon rare among marine gastropods, especially among such large ones. For all their considerable size these unusual whelks are not highly prized by collectors. It was a long time, however, before one of them, *Busycon coarctatum*, came on the market. For well over a century it was known only from a handful of unlocalized specimens in museums and was therefore much prized for its rarity. Then it was re-discovered about 1950 in the Yucatan area of the Gulf of Mexico. It is now worth very little. Re-discoveries of long-lost rarities like this are being announced each year in conchological journals, and

1 *Busycon contrarium* Conrad; 12·5 cm; S Carolina-Caribbean Prov. **2** *B. coarctatum* Sowerby; 13·0 cm; Gulf of Mexico. **3** *Bullia vittata* L.; 4·0 cm; Indian Ocean. **4** *B. vittata* showing the water-charged foot

soon after the discoveries are announced the re-discovered species may lose much of their glamour and most of their commercial value.

Bullias (Buccinacea)

Certainly *Bullia vittata* never was and never shall be considered a rarity, since it is a very common species in the Indian Ocean. It also has no pretension to beauty. This species is particularly abundant in the littoral zone of the Madras coast where it feeds voraciously on little crabs. It envelops a crab in its muscular mantle folds and clings so tightly to its victim that it will allow you to pull it almost out of its shell before letting go. It absorbs, through pores in its large foot, a great deal of water until it becomes bloated. By compressing its foot water is squirted out in various directions, to the endless amusement of many children of Madras. At low tide on a level beach the receding waves uncover large numbers of *Bullia vittata* engaged in obtaining food by burrowing below the sand surface. In order to regain their feeding positions they wave their water-charged foot in the air and then twist it over to secure a firm grip on the

3

4

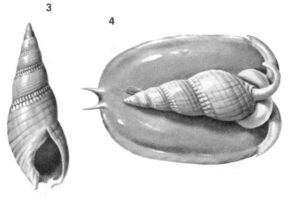

sand. The shell is then pulled over with a jerk into its original position. As soon as this position has been achieved the mollusc is ready to burrow beneath the surface of the sand again.

Babylon shells and others (Buccinacea)

Few gastropods are as heavy for their size as the babylon shells. Perhaps this is why the animals inhabiting them are usually so slow in their movements, although they are quick to sense danger and rapidly retreat within their shells when alarmed. In life their shells are covered by a thin, dirty-brown periostracum. In immature shells the umbilicus is visible but with age the inner lip thickens and eventually spreads over the site of the umbilicus. Siphonalia shells are carnivorous and are pests of oyster beds. The Netted Dog-whelk is carnivorous too and it is instructive to see how quickly it frightens off other molluscs when placed with them in an aquarium; scallop shells flit about in alarm as soon as one is placed near them.

Latirus shells (Buccinacea)

Several species of the genus *Latirus* have shells which can

1 *Cyrtulus serotinus* Hinds; 6·5 cm; Central Pacific. **2** Netted Dog Whelk, *Nassarius reticulatus* L.; 3·0 cm (shell only); Boreal-Mediterranean Provs. **3** *Siphonalia signum* Reeve; 4·0 cm; Japan. **4** *Latirus iris* Lightfoot, in the natural state; 3·6 cm; Pacific. **5** *L. iris*, wetted. **6** *Babylonia spirata* L.; 4·0 cm; Indian Ocean. **7** *B. zeylandica* Bruguière; 6·6 cm (shell only); Indian Ocean. Shell is shown without its brown periostracum

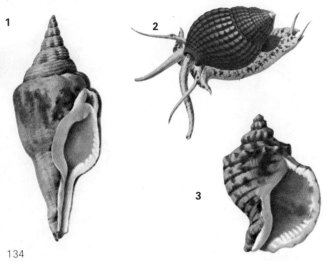

put on a display of iridescence. The phenomenon is best witnessed in shells of *Latirus iris* and was first noted by the eighteenth-century English conchologist Thomas Martyn who described it in these words: 'A very singular appearance, hitherto never observed of any other shell, is produced on this, by dipping it in water. The many small risings, or ribs of the shell, from a brown, are in a few moments changed to a rich and lucid blue, which beautiful effect again gradually dies away, as the shell becomes dry'. The artist can hardly do justice to the deep azure-blue iridescence which emanates from a wetted specimen. Remove the periostracum and the iridescent property is removed too. Apart from four or five related species this phenomenon is unknown in any other mollusc. No one knows if this iridescent quality serves any useful purpose for the animal. Protective resemblance to certain iridescent algae has been suggested but experimental evidence is lacking.

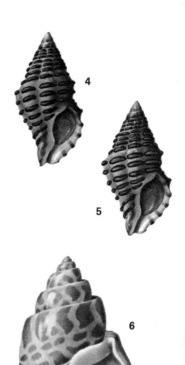

4

5

6

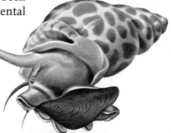

7

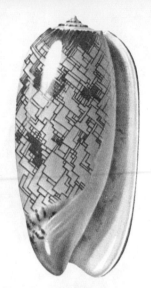

1 Tent Olive, *Oliva porphyria* L.; 6·5 cm; Panamic Prov. **2** *O. splendidula* Sowerby; 4·6 cm; Panamic Prov. **3** *Cancilla filaris* L.; 4·0 cm; Indo-Pacific Prov. **4** *Mitraria fissurata* Lamarck; 3·7 cm; Indian Ocean. **5** *Vexillum sanguisugum* L.; 4·8 cm; Indo-Pacific Prov. **6** *Vasum crosseanum* Souverbie; 6·1 cm; Seychelles

Olives (Volutacea)

For no obvious reason olives, which are restricted to warm waters and are abundant in the tropics, are not as popular with collectors as cowries. As the shells of both are glossy, smooth and colourful, equally strong and durable, it is possible that there is something less attractive to human eyes about the overall shape of olives. A contributory factor may be the lack of recognized rarities among them compared with the considerable number recognized among cowries. The popularity of the Tent Olive, however, has never been doubted. This, the largest of all olives and the principal conchological gem of the Panamic Province, owes its name to the numerous triangular markings or 'tents' which beset the entire body whorl. Olives are carnivorous but are indifferent to the condition of their meat and will consume it living or dead. They are very active at night and may then be seen suffocating their prey with their large foot. Usually they move along under the sand at a depth of one or two centimetres. Their eyes, which are very poorly developed, are situated about mid-way along the tentacles.

Mitres and vase shells (Volutacea)

Mitres are much more numerous in species than are the olives and there may be at least 500 different kinds living today. Nearly all of them are found in the tropics and most of them frequent sandy banks and lagoons; others may be found under coral blocks and in crevices on coral reefs. Some are particularly abundant close to human habitations in the tropics where the plentiful supply of offal offers a ready inducement to them to congregate. Like olives they are carnivorous and some have been observed smothering prey with their well-developed foot, just like olives do. One or two large species, when disturbed, have been seen to discharge a dark purple mucus which can stain cloth. The mucus is probably produced for defensive purposes and is presumably noxious to certain organisms (though harmless to humans). Mitres differ from olives by having their eyes near the base of the tentacles, but they resemble them in being devoid of an operculum. Vase shells are abundant in tropical waters, but two or three species are seldom seen in collections. Rarest of all is *Vasum crosseanum*, only two mature specimens having been recorded so far.

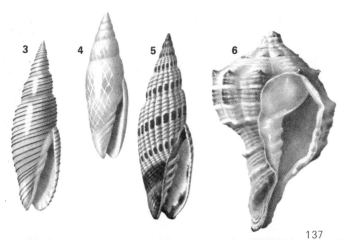

3 4 5 6

The Indian Chank (Volutacea)

It would appear unlikely that a mollusc should strongly influence the lives of countless persons to whom it has little or no appeal as an article of food; and yet the Indian Chank has done so for centuries. No other shell in the world has

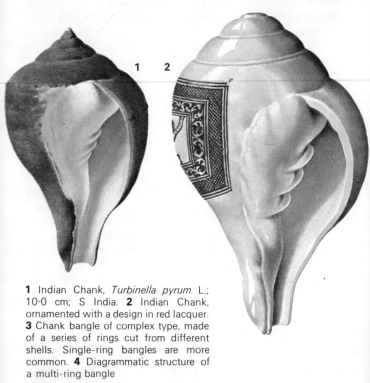

1 Indian Chank, *Turbinella pyrum* L.; 10·0 cm; S India. **2** Indian Chank, ornamented with a design in red lacquer. **3** Chank bangle of complex type, made of a series of rings cut from different shells. Single-ring bangles are more common. **4** Diagrammatic structure of a multi-ring bangle

gathered around it so much legend and folk-lore. A large species found only around the coasts of India and the Andaman Islands, its thick and heavy shell lends itself to the manufacture of several different kinds of artifacts. Libation vessels and engraved pendants fashioned from these shells have been unearthed from archaeological sites in the Indus Valley and Mesopotamia dating from the third millenium BC and in other forms Indian Chanks have continued to feature prominently in the lives of millions of Hindus. At birth a Hindu baby is often given a chank bangle or necklace, and a small shell may be used as a feeding bottle. When two Hindus marry, chank trumpets are blown to celebrate the event, the bride having put on a pair of lacquered chank bangles instead of a wedding ring. A complete shell may be buried in the foundations of a new home. The blowing of a chank trumpet usually celebrates a joyful or propitious event. It is also blown during acts of worship. Perhaps the shell came to have a religious significance because, as a trumpet, it can produce a lot of noise; and superstitious

3   4

peoples often believe that evil spirits can be scared away by loud noises. Many Bengalese still sound chank trumpets during an eclipse in the belief that they thereby put to flight the evil spirit which threatens to engulf the sun or the moon.

The Indian Chank's supposed powers are multiplied a thousandfold if the shell is a left-handed (sinistral) abnormality. Large and fine specimens of the sinistral form are exceedingly scarce and correspondingly valuable (they were once worth literally their weight in gold – and that sometimes meant a lot of gold). They still command high prices because of the widely held Hindu superstition that they bring prosperity to the owners. About two to three million Indian Chanks are fished annually in the waters of southern India, but it is unlikely that more than 200 sinistral specimens of high quality exist in that country even now.

Harps and spiny whelks (Volutacea)

The harp shells are easily distinguished from other kinds by their well-defined ribs and usually bright colour patterns. The close-set ribs of *Harpa costata* L., a Mauritian species, have made it a collector's favourite, and fine specimens always bring good prices at auctions. *Harpa major* is a common Indian Ocean species which may be seen for sale in curio shops along the coast of East Africa. The animal has a disconcerting habit of chopping off the end of its foot to avoid capture, and when its would-be captor is a human it almost invariably does so. There is a groove towards the posterior end of the foot and it is here that the animal detaches the deeper-coloured end portion. Sometimes it even leaves the fleshy lobe behind without provocation. This activity – rather like a man chopping off one of his own limbs – does not harm the creature at all and it soon grows a replacement for the missing portion. Spiny whelks resemble murex shells in some respects but they are in no sense close relatives.

1 *Trigonostoma pellucida* Perry; 2·5 cm; Indo-Pacific Prov. **2** *Tudicula armigera* A. Adams; 6·8 cm; Australia. **3** *Marginella pseudofaba* Sowerby; 3·2 cm; W African Prov. **4** *M. diadochus* Adams & Reeve; 2·3 cm (shell only); S African Prov. **5** *Harpa major* Röding; 7·0 cm (shell only); Indo-Pacific Prov. **6** *H. davidis* Röding; 7·0 cm; Indo-Pacific Prov

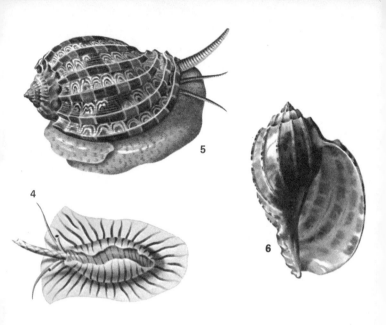

Nutmegs and margin shells (Volutacea)

Although nutmegs are undoubtedly attractive and form a well-defined group they are not numerous in private collections. Most of the species are concentrated in tropical waters off the western coast of America and these are the species most often acquired by collectors. The most desirable of all is *Trigonostoma pellucida* which appears to be widespread in the Indo-Pacific, but as no-one has yet found a productive locality for it it is still remarkably scarce and most of the larger museums have only one or two each. Many different kinds of margin shells are known from warm waters all around the globe and in some places beaches may be littered with millions of them. *Afrivoluta pringlei* Tomlin, which lives off the Natal coast, is so large that it was described originally as a volute. West Africa, however, is the best hunting ground for margin shells and an enterprising collector would be almost certain to find one or two species new to science there, especially if he hires a boat and dredges for them.

Volutes (Volutacea)

It has often been noted that molluscs which are very active crawlers are, in general, those whose shells have the richest colours. This is certainly true of volutes. The animals inhabiting some of the shells are also beautifully coloured, the patterns on shell and animal forming an arresting combination. Like so many highly coloured molluscs they are carnivorous and live on molluscs and other small organisms, smothering them in the folds of their large foot. Included in the group are some of the world's larger shells; some reach a length of 45 cm, and none is really small. Only a few live outside the tropics and of these *Ampulla priamus* has long been a collector's item. It is around the coasts of Australia, particularly in the vicinity of coral reefs, that most of the many different species live. New species are still being dredged up from deeper

1 *Harpeola kurodai* Kawamura; 7·3 cm; Taiwan. 2 Bednall's Volute, *Volutoconus bednalli* Brazier; 7·6 cm; NE Australia. 3 *Ampulla priamus* Gmelin; 6·0 cm; Spain, Portugal. 4 *Lyria anna* Lesson; 4·7 cm; Indo-Pacific Prov. 5 *Iredalina aurantia* Powell; 10·0 cm; N. Zealand

1

2

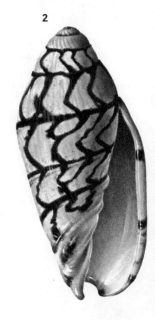

waters there by fishing vessels; and as volutes and some other seashells are commercially valuable – one shell can be worth as much as a whole cargo of fish – the fishermen sometimes forego normal fishing and concentrate on dredging for shells. Perhaps the most admired, and certainly the most readily identified, of all volutes is Bednall's Volute which is occasionally found in the waters off north-eastern Australia. Described in 1879 it is as desirable now as it was then, and is still beyond the means of most collectors to purchase. A later discovery *Iredalina aurantia* is noteworthy for its creamy orange colouring and complete absence of colour pattern. *Harpeola kurodai,* described in 1964, differs from both of these by its strong longitudinal ribs and deep suture. *Lyria anna,* less rare than these, is also strongly ribbed. Any one of these species, and many volutes besides, would have pride of place in a private collection.

If the words 'elegant' or 'graceful' are used to describe a shell it is probable that the shell described is a volute. This is particularly true of long, slender species which lack protuberances of any

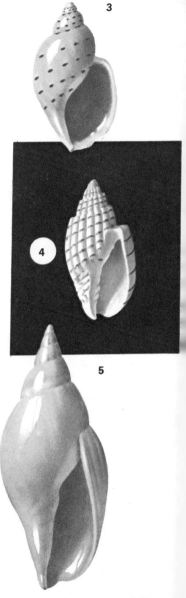

3

4

5

kind. Some species bearing spines or other processes on the shell are also very attractive. One of the commoner of these is the Bat Volute of the Indian Ocean, so called because of the fancied resemblance to the claws on a bat's wing. Most of the costly and desirable species, however, are smooth-shelled.

Baler shells (Volutacea)

The most spectacular volutes are known as melon or baler shells and have very large, globose shells and enormous bodies. The Great Barrier Reef and other coral reef areas in the warmest parts of the Pacific Ocean support several species, the common Australian one being *Melo amphora*. Its shell varies a great deal, and the prominent spines developed on young shells may be almost completely worn down on mature ones. It feeds on other molluscs and is especially fond of large bivalves. The voluminous foot is used to smother a bivalve until it opens its valves. Then its snout-like proboscis armed with rough radular teeth tears away at the victim's flesh until all the meaty parts are devoured. Baler shells, as their name implies, have been used for baling out water from canoes, and they have also been made into effective water carriers by natives of north-eastern Australia. In keeping with their great size they lay many eggs which

1 *Amoria canaliculata* McCoy; 5·0 cm; (shell only); E Australia. **2** Bat Volute, *Aulica vespertilio* L.; 8·5 cm; SW Pacific. **3** *Melo amphora* Lightfoot; 15·0 cm; Indo-Pacific Prov

1

2

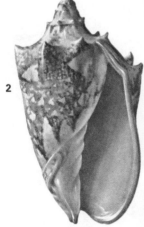

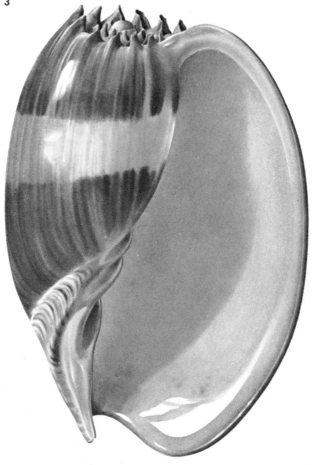

are encased in capsules and incorporated into a horny structure which may be larger than the parent animal. It takes so long for the eggs to be deposited that the mollusc carries it about attached to itself for many weeks, and the first-laid eggs are ready to hatch shortly after the egg-laying process has ended. As is usual with creatures which lay large numbers of eggs only a few will survive to maturity.

Turrids (Conacea)

On shell characters alone the rest of the molluscs described in this book are a very mixed bunch, but each group shares a singular anatomical peculiarity which sets it apart from all other molluscs: each includes species whose radula is used as an efficient and venomous harpoon. A long pointed tooth at the end of an extensible proboscis is connected to a poison gland in the animal's body and the whole apparatus may be used, sometimes with deadly effect, as a weapon of defence or offence. In the cones this venom apparatus may even represent danger to humans, but turrids are not so powerfully armed and some are without such an apparatus.

1 *Thatcheria mirabilis* Angas; 7·5 cm; Japan, N Australia. **2** *Clavatula imperialis* Lamarck; 5·3 cm; W African Prov. **3** *Turris babylonia* L.; 6·0 cm; Indo-Pacific Prov. **4** *Pusionella nifat* Bruguière; 4·5 cm; W African Prov. **5** *Gemmula cosmoi* Sykes; 5·5 cm; Japan, S African Prov. **6** *Conorbis coromandelicus* Smith; 4·6 cm; Indian Ocean

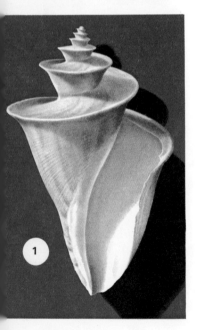

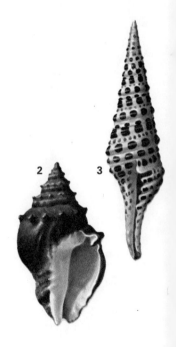

A prominent distinguishing feature of turrids is the sinus, or anal notch, which may be seen at the top of the outer lip. Broadly speaking it corresponds in function to the row of holes in an abalone's shell and to the single hole in the shell of a keyhole limpet. Though prominent in some species it is scarcely perceptible in others.

Turrids are highly evolved creatures and their shells are known from geological deposits at least a hundred million years old. They form a very successful group, there being many different species. They are found in shallow water as well as in the abyssal depths and are present in all the world's seas. Relatively few are colourful, and the colour pattern of *Turris babylonia* is about the most striking to be found in the whole group, most species being dull white or brownish. *Thatcheria mirabilis* is undoubtedly the largest and the most admired of all the turrids and is generally considered to be one of the most exquisitely shaped gastropods in the world.

Auger shells (Conacea)
With the exception of the screw shells (page 98) no

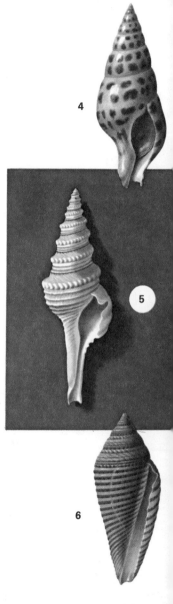

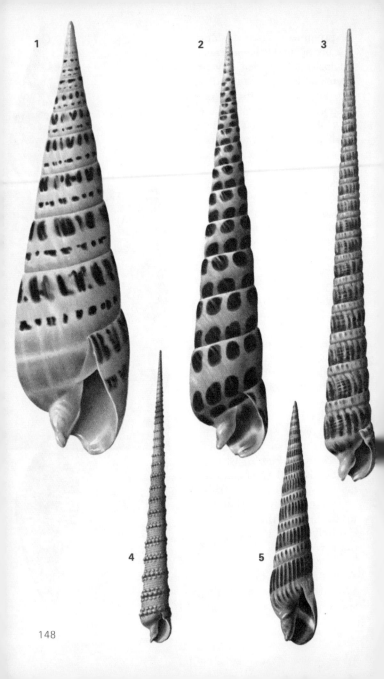

other molluscs resemble augers (so called because they look like boring tools and may be utilized as such). All have long, many-whorled shells and many of them are elaborately sculptured and strikingly patterned. The operculum is claw-shaped, unlike that of the screw shells which is circular. All of the colourful species are inhabitants of warm seas and the finest specimens are found in the vicinity of coral reefs. The deep-water forms are usually sombre-hued. Most shallow-water species live in sandy habitats – such attenuated shells would be smashed to pieces in a rocky environment – and usually they move about just below the sand surface leaving behind them a characteristic ridged track. The animal may be surprisingly strong and can burrow downwards leaving the long siphon in contact with the surface. It might be thought that such long and relatively heavy shells would restrict the movements of the animals which carry them, but this does not seem to be so. Most of the weight is concentrated in the basal portion, which is where the bulk of the animal is too, and so it is sometimes possible for the animal to crawl along with its shell sloping or even erect. It is noticeable that shells with spiral ridges on the columella are attached to their animals by powerful muscles, and most auger shells have a single spiral ridge. The largest species, and one of the commoner, is *Terebra maculata* which is normally about 15 cm long. As in many tropical molluscs giant specimens are found among the augers and the world-record length for a specimen of *T. maculata* is just over 25 cm! This species is smooth all over and glossy; but many species, such as *T. dussumieri*, are longitudinally ribbed. A granulated sculpture encircling the whorls characterizes *T. triseriata* which is otherwise remarkable for its extremely slender form. A mature specimen of this species with all its whorls intact is a rare find and such specimens have always been in demand among collectors. *T. pretiosa*, another collector's item, is one of the finest and least variable species in the group.

1 *Terebra maculata* L.; 15·0 cm; Indo-Pacific Prov. **2** *T. subulata* L.; 12·5 cm; Indo-Pacific Prov. **3** *T. pretiosa* Reeve; 13·5 cm; Pacific. **4** *T. triseriata* Gray; 9·0 cm; Indo-Pacific Prov. **5** *T. dussumieri* Kiener; 7·7 cm; Pacific

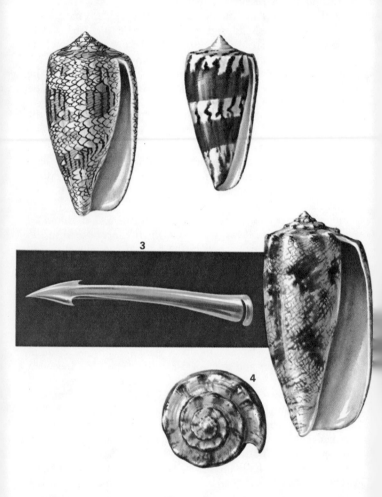

1 *Conus textile* L.; 8·8 cm; Indo-Pacific Prov. **2** *C. generalis* L.; 6·5 cm; Indo-Pacific Prov. **3** Tooth of *C. geographus* highly magnified. **4** *C. geographus* L.; 10·0 cm; Indo-Pacific Prov. **5** *C. marmoreus* L.; 9·0 cm; Indo-Pacific Prov. **6** *C. augur* Lightfoot; 5·0 cm; Indo-Pacific Prov

Cones (Conacea)

These have always been among the most desirable of shells and there are so many different kinds that no person or institution owns examples of all of them. Like the cowries they conform to a single, immediately recognizable shape but vary enormously in colour and colour pattern. In size they range from 1 cm to 30 cm. Most of them are found in the warm waters of the Indo-Pacific Province and usually they occur in fairly shallow water, sometimes in abundance.

The collector of cones must realize that several species are killers, of humans as well as fishes. They manufacture a potent poison which is injected into the prey (or the prying human hand) to paralyse it. Small fishes succumb immediately and are swallowed whole; humans usually survive but nearly always experience some pain and often extreme agony. A recent survey showed that of thirty-seven known cases of cone stings ten ended fatally. All the fatalities were probably attributable to two species, *Conus geographus* and *C. textile*, although twelve other species are known to have inflicted painful wounds on humans. In 1960 an adult male died within two hours of being stung by a *C. geographus* at Koumac, New Caledonia. A needle-like tooth, hollow from end to end, is shot into the prey and a paralysing fluid, stored in a special sac, is injected through it and into the wound. As the tooth is replaceable the cone can repeat the process many times. There is no known antidote. Obviously the chances of being killed by a cone are remote. There are perhaps 350 to 400 species of *Conus* living today and the beauty of most of them compensates for the lethal properties of a few.

5

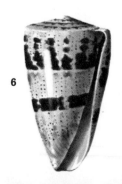
6

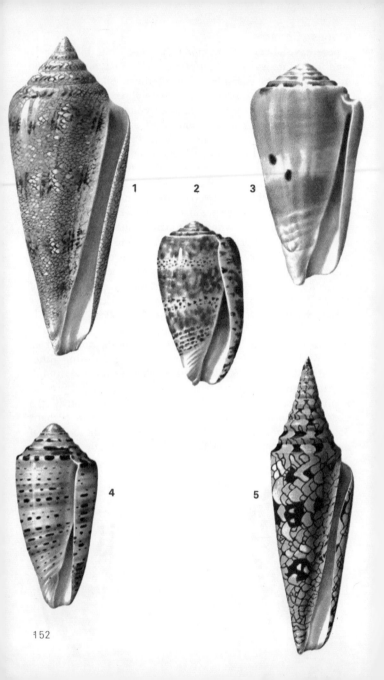

1   2   3

4

5

Rare cones

Perhaps only one seashell in the world can truly be considered newsworthy: the Glory-of-the-Sea Cone. Until very recently it was the most desirable shell known, for the sinistral Indian Chank is desired less for itself than for the powers which it is supposed to possess. The Glory-of-the-Sea Cone was first recorded over two centuries ago but up to 1957 only two dozen specimens had been found. Now that over one hundred specimens are known and new localities have been discovered off New Britain and elsewhere in the Pacific, it is no longer the undisputed idol of collectors. Nonetheless it still commands a high price. For one of the finest specimens known an American collector paid $2,000 in 1964 (certain cowries and volutes have been sold for much more than this subsequently). Scarcity combined with a compelling name had helped to transform this shapely but not exceptionally beautiful species into a paragon among shells. It may be only a matter of time before it becomes commonplace, but time will never obliterate the legend that has clung to it for such a long time.

There are several cone shells which knowledgeable collectors would willingly take in preference to the Glory-of-the-Sea Cone. Of these the Glory-of-India Cone has a high priority, its remarkably elevated spire and vivid colour pattern attracting many covetous eyes. All the cones illustrated on the opposite page are practically unobtainable unless money is no object, and even then it would probably be necessary to resort to theft in order to aquire one or two of them. *Conus barthelemyi*, for instance, has been found only once or twice since 1861 when the original specimen (from which the accompanying illustration was painted) was described. Like most non-utilitarian things which we collect, shells may become notorious, and consequently desirable, if they are in very short supply.

1 Glory of the Sea, *Conus gloriamaris* Chemnitz; 9·8 cm; W Pacific. **2** *C. adamsonii* Broderip; 4·7 cm; Central Pacific. **3** *C. barthelemyi* Bernardi; 6·7 cm; Indian Ocean. **4** *C. aurisiacus* L.; 5·5 cm; Indo-Pacific Prov. **5** Glory of India, *C. milneedwardsi* Jousseaume; 9·6 cm; Indian Ocean

BUYING, EXCHANGING AND IDENTIFYING SHELLS

Wherever you live you will probably want to own specimens from places you are unable to visit. Such specimens may be obtained by purchase or exchange. Shells may be bought from several sources, including auction houses and curio shops, but many are readily obtainable only from dealers. Most dealers issue price lists regularly and give satisfactory service, but it is wise to check with other collectors before patronizing any dealer of unknown reputation. Shells bought at auction are usually expensive, but an expert with money to spare can pick up bargains occasionally. The beginner will find auction sales fascinating and instructive but he should resist the temptation to join in the bidding; he may pick up a rare shell at a bargain price, but he is more likely to go away with a box of attractive but expensive rubbish. Perhaps the most satisfactory – certainly the cheapest – way to build up your shell collection is by exchange. Almost any shells in good condition and well labelled with locality data may be offered for others. Shells which seem to you to be common and worthless may be gathered profitably because they will not be common in other countries.

If you have something to offer it is not difficult to enter into exchange with other collectors. By joining one of the world's numerous shell clubs you are automatically brought into contact with other collectors who will exchange shells with you and offer useful advice. A few shell clubs are listed opposite. Many others are listed in *Van Nostrand's Standard Catalog of Shells*. The natural history department of any large museum should be able to help you locate a suitable shell club. It is also reasonable to expect help from the conchologist of a large museum, but do not expect too much and do not expect anything if you have not made an appointment. Do not take a large collection of undocumented shells to him hoping for spot identifications of the lot. It is best to ask him to identify only two or three shells at any one time. Remember, too, that he cannot possibly know every described species on sight. Try to identify your shells with the aid of books. Those listed on page 156 give illustrations and descriptions of many of the shells you are likely to own. The *Sheller's Directory* by T. C. Rice gives a compendious list of clubs, dealers, books and periodicals. The *Directory of Conchologists* by R. E. Petit lists collectors and students from all over the world and indicates their respective interests. When sending shells through the post pack them very carefully. Always treat your shells as though they were precious pieces of porcelain.

Shell clubs around the world

The following brief list is a small selection of clubs, membership of which is open to anyone interested in shells.

Association of Philippine Shell Collectors, Inc., Manila, Philippines.
Centre Français de Malacologie sur la Côte d'Azur, Nice 06, France.
Conchiglia Club de Milano, 73 Via de Sanctis, Milan, Italy.
Conchological Club of Southern California, Los Angeles, California, U.S.A.
Conchological Society of Great Britain and Ireland, London, England.
Conchological Society of Southern Africa, South African Museum, Cape Town, South Africa.
Fiji Shell Club, Suva, Fiji.
Fondation Conchyliologique de Belgique, Genese, Belgium.
Gloria Maris Association of Shell Collectors, Antwerp, Belgium.
Hawaiian Malacological Society, Honolulu, Hawaii.
Keppel Bay Shell Club, Yeppoon, Queensland, Australia.
Malacological Society of Australia, Australian Museum, Sydney, Australia.
Malacological Society of Japan, Tokyo, Japan.
Marianas Shell Club, Tipalo, Guam Island, Marianas.
Nederlandse Malacologische Vereniging, The Hague, Netherlands.
New York Shell Club, New York, U.S.A.
New Zealand Shell Club, Auckland, New Zealand.
Oregon Shell Club, Portland, Oregon, U.S.A.
Port Denison Shell Club, Queensland, Australia.
Sociedad Malacologica del Uruguay, Montevideo, Uruguay.
Western Australia Shell Club, Perth, Australia.

BOOKS TO READ

A Beginner's Guide to South African Shells by K. H. Barnard. Maskew Miller Ltd., Cape Town, 1953.

American Seashells by R. T. Abbott. D. Van Nostrand Co., Princeton, 1954.

Australian Shells by Joyce Allan. Georgian House, Melbourne, 1959.

British Bivalve Seashells by N. Tebble. British Museum (Natural History), London, 1966.

British Prosobranch Molluscs by V. Fretter and A. Graham. Ray Society, London, 1962.

British Shells by N. F. McMillan. Frederick Warne and Co. Ltd., London, 1968.

Caribbean Seashells by G. L. Warmke and R. T. Abbott. Livingston Publ. Co., Narberth, Pa., 1961.

Collecting Shells by S. M. Turk. W. and G. Foyle Ltd., London, 1966.

Coloured Illustrations of the Shells of Japan by T. Kira and T. Habe. Hoikushu Publ. Co., Osaka, (2 vols.) 1959 and 1961.

Directory of Conchologists by R. E. Petit. P.O. Box 133, Ocean Drive Beach, S. Carolina 29582, U.S.A., 1970.

Marine Shells of the Pacific by W. O. Cernohorsky. Pacific Publications, Sydney, 1967.

Molluscs by J. E. Morton. Hutchinson University Library, London, 1967.

Rare Shells by S. P. Dance. Faber, London, and Univ. California Press, Los Angeles, 1969.

Seashells of the World by R. T. Abbott. Golden Press, New York, 1962.

Seashells of the World, with Values by A. G. Melvin. Charles Tuttle Co., Rutland and Tokyo, 1966.

Sea Shells of Tropical West America by A. M. Keen. Stanford University Press, Stanford, 1958.

Shell Collecting: an Illustrated History by S. P. Dance. Faber, London, and University of California Press, Los Angeles, 1966.

Sheller's Directory of Clubs, Books, Periodicals and Dealers by T. C. Rice. Of Sea and Shore, P.O. Box 33, Port Gamble, Washington 98364, U.S.A., 1970.

Shells by R. C. Cameron. Weidenfeld and Nicolson, London, 1961.

Shells of New Zealand by A. W. B. Powell. Whitcombe and Tombs, Auckland, 1961.

Van Nostrand's Standard Catalog of Shells edited by R. J. L. Wagner and R. T. Abbott. D. Van Nostrand Co., Princeton, 1967.

INDEX

SOME OTHER TITLES IN THIS SERIES

Natural History

The Animal Kingdom
Animals of Australia & New Zealand
Animals of Southern Asia
Bird Behaviour
Birds of Prey
Butterflies
Evolution of Life
Fishes of the World
Fossil Man
A Guide to the Seashore
Life in the Sea
Mammals of the World
Monkeys and Apes
Natural History Collecting
The Plant Kingdom
Prehistoric Animals
Seabirds
Snakes of the World
Tropical Birds
Wild Cats

Gardening

Chrysanthemums
Garden Flowers
Garden Shrubs
House Plants
Plants for Small Gardens
Roses

Popular Science

Astronomy
Atomic Energy

Chemistry
Computers at Work
The Earth
Electricity
Electronics
Exploring the Planets
The Human Body
Mathematics
Microscopes & Microscopic Life
The Weather Guide

Arts

Antique Furniture
Architecture
Clocks and Watches
Glass for Collectors
Jewellery
Porcelain
Victoriana

General Information

Aircraft
Arms and Armour
Coins and Medals
Flags
Guns
Military Uniforms
Rockets and Missiles
Sailing
Sailing Ships & Sailing Craft
Sea Fishing
Trains
Veteran & Vintage Cars
Warships

● Natural History   ● Gardening

● Popular Science   ● Arts

● General Information   ● Domestic Animals & Pets

● Domestic Science   ● History & Mythology